FLOWER ARRANGING

A STEP-BY-STEP GUIDE TO FLORAL DESIGN

Wildflower.Media

PUBLISHER: Travis Rigby
AUTHOR: Teresa P. Lanker
EDITORS: Robin Avni, David Coake
FLORAL DESIGNERS: Teresa P. Lanker; Frank Feysa, AIFD
CONTRIBUTING FLORAL DESIGNERS: Heather Bauder, Beth Zsoldos
PHOTOGRAPHER: Todd Kaminski
CONSULTANT: Kelly Mace
PARTNERS: Smithers-Oasis North America
ART DIRECTOR: Kathleen Dillinger

Flower Arranging: A Step-by-step Guide to Floral Design was produced by WildFlower Media, Inc.
Topeka, Kansas. *floristsreview.com*

Printed in China

ISBN 978-1-7337826-2-3

INTRODUCTION

It's an interesting time in the floral industry. Design is changing, shifting, loosening up and expanding definitions. Designers are striving for greater floral artistry, with mixed media fusions of flowers, metals, wood and wire, while also relaxing into organic uses of garden-picked posies in shapes that defy familiar norms. Yet, the fundamentals of design haven't changed. The elements used to create arrangements and the principles that guide the process are the same. Likewise, the steps that assure a visually pleasing finished product remain tried and true.

This book is written as a foundation for the novice entering this new world of floristry. It also serves as a refresher for the experienced designer and as a springboard to the next level for designers in between. The ability to create emerging styles of design relies heavily on solid fundamentals. Mastering the classic round mound, the one-sided triangle, the horizontal centerpiece, the European hand-tied and one dozen roses in a vase is akin to learning the five mother sauces of classical cuisine. To be taken seriously, a designer must master these essentials of the craft.

As design styles shift, so too do the products at the designer's disposal. Understanding how to use these new products to ease the design process, secure mechanics and increase efficiency is vital to success. Assuring flowers are designed to maximize vase life potential is also critical. All the better when mechanics can be made both life-sustaining and decorative. Throughout this book, multiple approaches to mechanics are shared, providing the designer with a range of options for creating arrangements for common occasions and unique situations. Truly comprehensive, this book provides extensive visual examples and step-by-step instructions for designs that run the gamut from everyday to special occasions, new baby arrangements to sympathy sprays, flowers to wear and bouquets to carry. Instructions are provided for often overlooked areas of holiday and novelty design, providing the tricks and tips necessary to achieve polished results. Modern and approachable design concepts are also presented demonstrating inspirations from art and nature.

Success as a floral designer requires the ability to partner flowers with containers, colors with textures, ideas with reality, and more. It relies on the capacity to visualize a concept and carry it through to completion, and the knowledge to apply established principles to recommended processes. Success is made sweeter when results are given a personal stamp of originality or a new and creative spin. With effort and focus, these keys to success can be learned. May this book be your inspiration and guide to growth as an artisan of flowers.

TERESA LANKER
Author and Floral Designer
Teresa has spent her entire professional career in the floral industry starting with her first flower shop job at the age of 16 at Amling's Flowerland in the Chicago area. She has held positions as floral designer, event designer and retail florist manager. For more than 30 years, Teresa also serves as an educator of budding florists as associate professor and coordinator of the Floral Design and Marketing program at The Ohio State University in Wooster, Ohio.

In addition, Teresa serves as chair of the Ohio State ATI Horticulture Division. She holds a Bachelor of Science degree in Ornamental Horticulture and Master of Education degree, both from the University of Illinois. She has received university, state and national awards for outstanding teaching.

Teresa has presented floral design programs, seminars and hands-on workshops throughout the U.S. and has served on educational design teams and as an educational liaison for multiple florist groups. Her work has been featured in books, magazines and floral selection guides. She has authored numerous floral design publications including books, articles and educational resources. Her previous works for *Florists' Review* include the first edition of this book and *Modern Flower Arranging: Step-by-step Instructions for Modern Designs*.

FRANK FEYSA, AIFD, CFD, PFCI
Floral Designer
Frank has been involved in the floral industry for more than 30 years as a retail shop owner, event designer, educator and commercial print designer. He is past president of the American Institute of Floral Designers (AIFD) and served as chairman of the AIFD National Symposium "Transition/Transformation" in Chicago, Illinois.

In addition to his specialty floral event company, Frank currently works as a design director for the Smithers-Oasis Company and teaches commercial and contemporary floral design at The Ohio State University in Wooster, Ohio. His work has been featured in many industry publications and commercial ads. Frank has traveled extensively presenting design programs and hands-on workshops nationally and internationally on a wide variety of floral subjects.

TODD KAMINSKI
Photographer
Todd Kaminski is a commercial and architectural photographer based in Akron, Ohio. He has a strong background in fine art photography and more than 25 years of experience in commercial photography. He has been working with the floral industry for more than 20 years and believes every picture is an opportunity to create a unique work of art. His clients praise his technical skills, excellent customer service and, above all else, his flair for capturing true emotion in the photographs he produces.

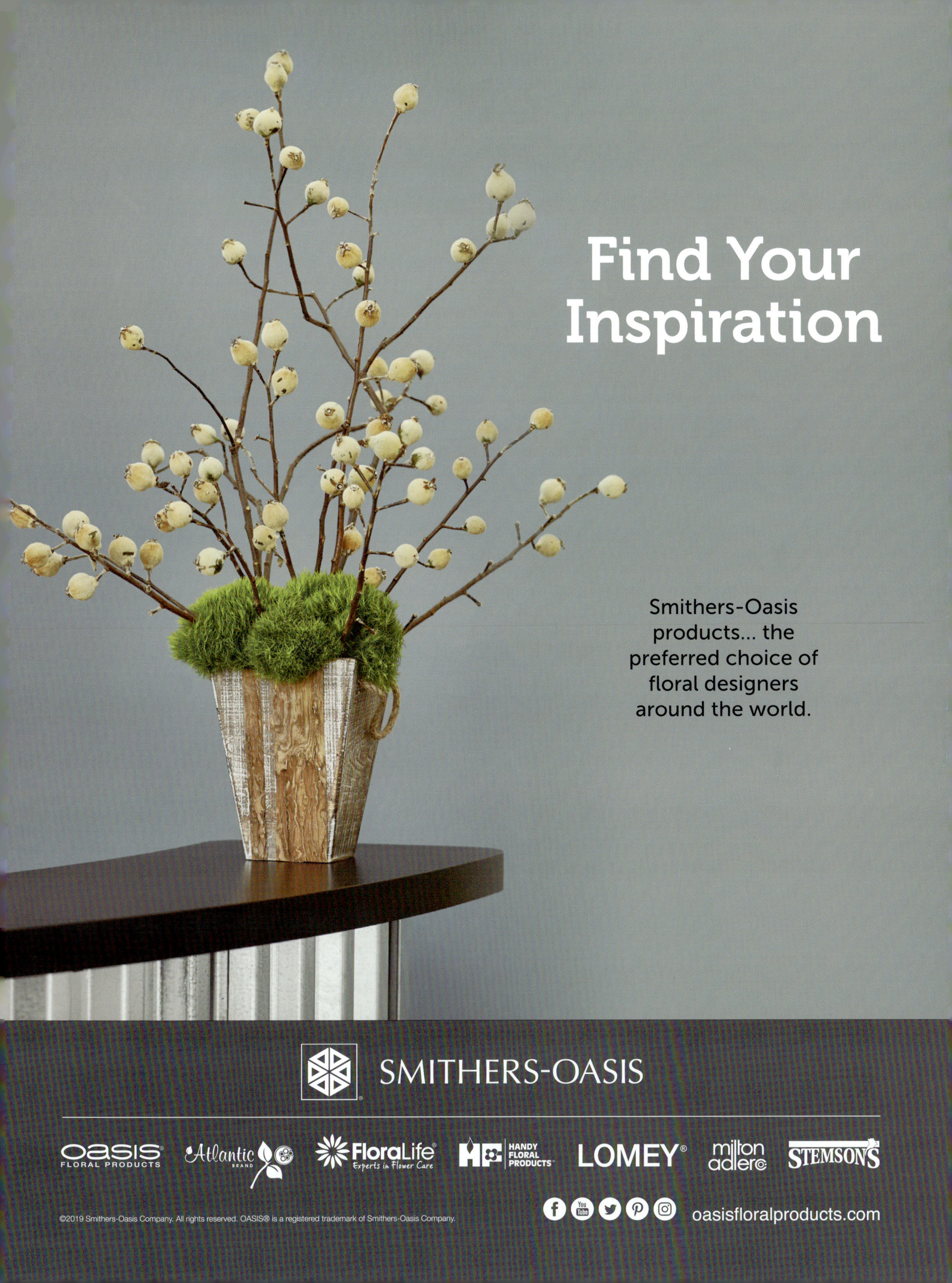

CONTENTS

Chapter One

PRINCIPLES & ELEMENTS

Floral design is an artistic process that relies on the presentation of flowers in an organized and aesthetically pleasing manner. Consideration and strategic use of the unique attributes of individual flowers, foliages, containers and accessories are essential. So, too, are the principles that guide the process of putting the design components together. The elements and principles of design are well documented, having universal application to a host of design fields including interior design, landscape design, graphic design and more. In this chapter, we highlight the key floral elements and methods of application of accepted floral design principles.

ELEMENTS OF FLORAL DESIGN

The elements of floral design are often described as the ingredients that make up a flower arrangement. They are the tangible aspects of the flowers, foliages and other design components that are selected and strategically combined by a designer.

Line

Line is often used to establish the overall outline or silhouette of an arrangement. It provides a dominant visual pathway for the eye to follow. Upright lines create a sense of formality while slanted or horizontal lines convey informality. Straight lines are often described as *static*. These lines can be stately, contributing a feeling of strength and stability, but they also can be stiff, which can lessen the visual energy of a design. Curved, arched, spiraled and contorted lines are more *dynamic*, meaning they have visual energy and add life to the party. The successful use of each of these types of lines relies on the thoughtful application of the principles of design, particularly balance and proportion.

Consider these tips when working with line:

- Extend lines to the maximum recommended proportion for the container of choice.
- Angle the top line of a design slightly backward to allow more opportunity for dimension from front to back.
- Angle horizontal lines slightly downward to reduce stiffness and increase unity with the container.
- Avoid overuse of dynamic lines to prevent a composition that appears "busy" or unfocused
- Position flowers and foliage to avoid crossing lines that confuse the eye.
- Combine two or more opposing lines in an arrangement, such as a vertical line and a crescent line, to add energy and create a greater sense of style.

This monobotanical orchid arrangement features a strong vertical line created by a contorted piece of curly willow, thus achieving strong visual energy despite the formal line placement.

Form

Form refers to the three-dimensional shape of flower arrangements. The outline created by the height, width and depth of flowers and foliage is the design form. Many floral design forms are based on geometric shapes. These styles are sometimes referred to as mass designs in reference to the volume of materials used to fill out their forms.

Common geometric mass design forms include:

- Circular
- Triangular
- Oblong
- Diamond
- Oval

Line-mass arrangements present a different collection of forms. Some are familiar shapes while others are more organic or irregular. Traditional examples include vertical, diagonal, crescent, Hogarth ("S" curve), inverted "T" and "L" shape while modern examples include vegetative, parallel systems, topiary and waterfall. The flowers and foliages used to create arrangements can also be categorized by their three-dimensional forms. See chart below.

Consider these tips when working with form:

- Envision the form you intend to achieve before you begin the design process.
- Establish the outline of the form first, then fill in the center.
- Implied forms can be created without completely defining the entire outline, resulting in a visually lighter composition.
- Extend flowers at the edge of the container forward to achieve dimension.
- Strive for variety, using a combination of line, mass, focal and filler materials to create interest.

The triangular form of this arrangement is achieved using larkspur to establish the tip and side points, carnations to fill out the form, and cremone chrysanthemums to add focal interest. *Hypericum*, statice and micro spray mums fill the gaps, adding color and texture, and creating a unified finished design.

Form	Description	Common Uses	Examples
Line	A spike-like flower or foliage, generally tall and narrow.	Used to establish the height of an arrangement or any outer points.	Larkspur, *Liatris*, Snapdragon, Stock, *Gladiolus*, Myrtle, Flax.
Mass	A solid round flower, typically with a dense concentration of petals.	Used to develop volume within an established design outline.	Carnation, Chrysanthemum, China Aster, 'Green Trick' *Dianthus*, *Hydrangea*.
Form (or Focal)	A flower of any uniquely decorative form that makes it particularly useful as a center of attention, thus the term focal flower.	Used as a primary element in the focal point or other featured area of a design.	Rose, Lily, Orchid, *Gerbera*, Sunflower, Calla, *Anthurium*, Bird-of-Paradise.
Filler	A flower or foliage typically dotted with small blooms, leaves, seeds or berries, creating a fluffy impact.	Used to fill open spaces between flowers and to add color or textural contrast.	Baby's Breath, Waxflower, *Solidago*, *Hypericum*, Statice, *Limonium*, Plumosa Fern, Seeded *Eucalyptus*.

Space

As an element of floral design, **space** includes both the area taken up by the design materials (referred to as *positive space*) and the open spaces between them (*negative space*). Some styles, such as the parallel systems design, have intentional gaps between areas or units. These gaps are referred to as *voids*.

The use of space in an arrangement should be deliberate. Good spacing contributes to good balance and maximizes the impact of the individual flowers. An essential design skill is the ability to visualize the finished composition and use flowers to fill the space that creates the desired form. For most designs, the spacing should transition from tip to center so that the flowers in the middle are closer together and those at the tips are farther apart. Some arrangements, such as the round mound, are intentionally spaced with the flowers close together. This creates the desired compact mounded result. The same arrangement, when designed with more open spacing can look like an entirely different design.

Consider these tips when working with space:

- Allow enough space between flowers to avoid crowding, which diminishes the shapes or otherwise damages individual blooms.
- Consider spacing that implies butterflies could flutter through the top or perimeter.
- Too much space between elements may weaken the unity of the design.
- Avoid a space or gap between the flowers and the container in order to assure a sufficient union.
- A crowded design uses more materials, many of which are wasted if they cannot be seen.
- Space is free, so use it liberally to enhance designs without adding cost.

This design makes a big statement using only four tulip stems thanks to the tremendous negative space between the blooming branches.

Size

Another tangible element under the control of the designer is **size**. Size is simply the area taken up by the flowers, container and overall composition. When designing for commercial purposes, generally, the bigger the design can be made with given materials, the better. This results in a greater perceived value, the impression of how much an arrangement is worth monetarily. As demonstrated in the four-tulip arrangement on the previous page, an extended line combined with well-managed space can create the impression of a sizable design using minimal materials.

Consider these tips when working with size:

- Consider the setting, container size and intended use to help determine appropriate design size.
- Choose flowers and foliage with suitable stem length to achieve the desired size.
- Use increased height and spacing between flowers to expand the size of an arrangement.
- Recognize petite and delicate flowers that would be lost within a sizable arrangement and save them for more diminutive designs.

Color

Of all the floral design elements, **color** has, arguably, the greatest influence on a viewer's response to an arrangement. More than the flowers, container or design style, most often, the initial reaction to a floral arrangement is based on color. Color preferences are highly varied and decidedly personal. Most people have a favorite color and one or more colors they dislike. Still, there are many colors that are enjoyed when they are the right tint, tone or shade, or are combined with other "right" colors.

Effective use of color is learned with experience. Like other aspects of design, with practice, the eyes become more discerning and the designer more skillful in putting colors together. There are many art books and floral design resources that provide foundational knowledge of color. These can be very helpful in developing an understanding of the intricacies of how light reflected from an object to the eyes is observed as color. Here, we focus on terminology and color harmonies that are most useful when working with color to create pleasing flower arrangements.

Primary, Secondary and Tertiary Colors

A quick study of the color wheel reveals the *primary* (red, yellow, blue) and *secondary* colors (orange, green and violet), and the *tertiary* colors that fall in between. Also known as intermediate, tertiary colors combine one primary and one secondary color, resulting in six additional colors: red-orange, red-violet, yellow-orange, yellow-green, blue-violet and blue-green.

The color wheel can be divided into warm and cool colors. The *warm* colors of red, orange and yellow are sometimes referred to as advancing colors. Visually, they advance toward the viewer, conveying strength, power and authority. These colors are attention seekers and can overpower other colors, even in small doses.

The *cool* colors of green, blue and violet are more quiet. Sometimes referred to as receding colors, they are calm, peaceful and restful. When paired with warm colors, they can easily blend into the background. Thoughtful proportions are needed when warm and cool colors are combined so both contribute to a pleasing result.

Tints, Tones and Shades

The term *hue* is used to describe the base from which an object's color originated. Red, orange, yellow, green, blue and violet are hues. Black, white and gray are devoid of color, thus they are considered *neutrals*. When these neutrals are added to a hue in varying amounts, any number of colors can be created, each with a different *value*, a term used to describe its lightness or darkness. The addition of white creates *tints*, the addition of gray creates *tones*, and the addition of black creates *shades*. Using the red hue as an example, adding white creates pink, adding gray creates mauve, and adding black creates burgundy. A color's *intensity* (or *chroma*), is its brightness or dullness. A pure hue is said to be fully saturated. In this state, it has maximum intensity. When it is combined with other colors, or is mixed with gray, its intensity is lessened.

Color Harmonies

An eye for color is a defining attribute of an accomplished floral designer. For many, the art of combining colors is learned through diligent practice and a healthy dose of trial and error. A key source of inspiration and direction comes from the study and use of established color harmonies. For a beginning designer, a randomly created color scheme may or may not be successful, but a color scheme based on tried-and-true combinations has a greater likelihood of success.

As the name implies, color harmonies provide a guide to combining colors into pleasing, harmonious combinations. By using these harmonies and varying the values, proportions and placements of the combined colors, the possibilities are endless. Here, we highlight the common color harmonies employed by floral designers.

Achromatic

Achromatic color harmonies are devoid of color. They include any combination of white, black and gray. Often, in floral design, achromatic arrangements are made primarily or entirely of white flowers. Gray and blackish foliages and flowers in very deep shades of plum provide opportunities for contrast within the achromatic harmony. As is true of the color schemes of most floral arrangements, the color green is treated as a neutral when supplied by the foliage or other green flower parts. The absence of color in an achromatic design increases the need for variety among the flower forms and textures.

Monochromatic

A *monochromatic* color harmony features only one hue but may include multiple tints, tones and shades of that hue. A common monochromatic color harmony from the violet hue includes the colors eggplant (shade), lilac (tone) and lavender (tint). The monochromatic harmony combining light pink, mid-pink and hot pink, is popular for baby arrangements. Orange and peach combine to make a cheerful summer harmony. Typically, colors are mixed within arrangements, but an ombré effect can be created within a monochromatic color harmony by grouping the lightest tints at the perimeter, the deepest shades at the base and the tones in between so the colors fade one into another progressing from light to dark.

Cymbidium orchids and 'Monte Cassino' *Aster* combine in this simple all-white *achromatic* design. Asymmetrical flower placements within a mass design form and contrasting textures provided by neutral foliage and filler elements add a level of complexity that elevates interest despite the simplicity and petite proportions.

A *monochromatic* Phoenix-style arrangement makes a strong statement using a variety of flower and foliage forms. Lime green, gray-green and mid-green elements provide pleasant contrasts while the creamy variegation of the flax adds a striped pattern that creates excitement.

Analogous

An *analogous* color harmony combines any three hues side by side on the color wheel. Possible combinations include one primary and two adjacent tertiary colors; one secondary and two adjacent tertiary colors; and one primary color, one secondary color and the tertiary color in between. The analogous color harmony of yellow, yellow-orange and orange is popular for fall arrangements. Blue, blue-violet and violet is a peaceful color harmony for sympathy arrangements. Analogous colors provide low risk combinations. Use them to tie to a known color when you have limited information about a situation, setting or color preference.

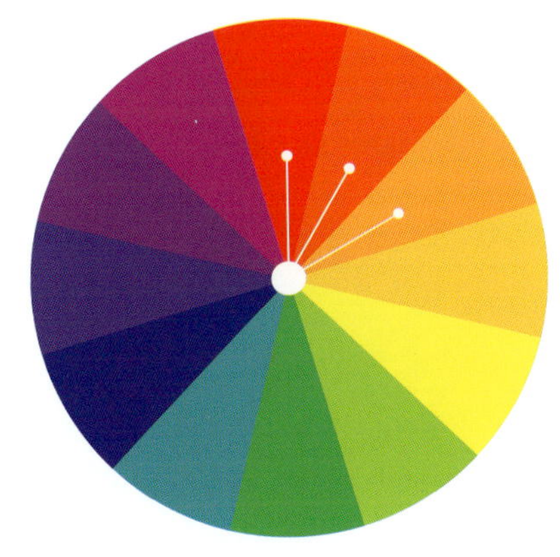

(Analogous continued)
Neighbors on the color wheel, yellow and orange combine in this simple *analogous* color harmony comprising golden yellow daisy spray mums, tangerine spray carnations and peachy spray *Alstroemeria*.

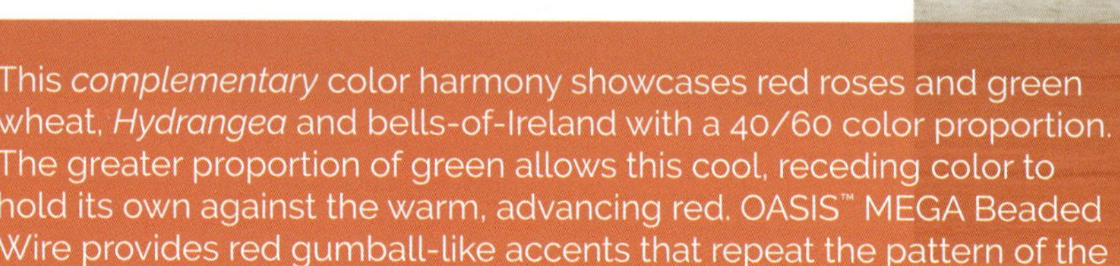

This *complementary* color harmony showcases red roses and green wheat, *Hydrangea* and bells-of-Ireland with a 40/60 color proportion. The greater proportion of green allows this cool, receding color to hold its own against the warm, advancing red. OASIS™ MEGA Beaded Wire provides red gumball-like accents that repeat the pattern of the polka-dotted container.

Complementary

Complementary colors are contrasting hues located directly across from each other on the color wheel. Each of the primary colors and their secondary complements provide the familiar complementary harmonies of red/green, yellow/violet and blue/orange. These combinations pair a warm and a cool color together, often with striking results. Complementary tertiary colors, such as red-orange paired with blue-green are less familiar combinations and may require strategic use of tints, tones and shades to enhance their appeal.

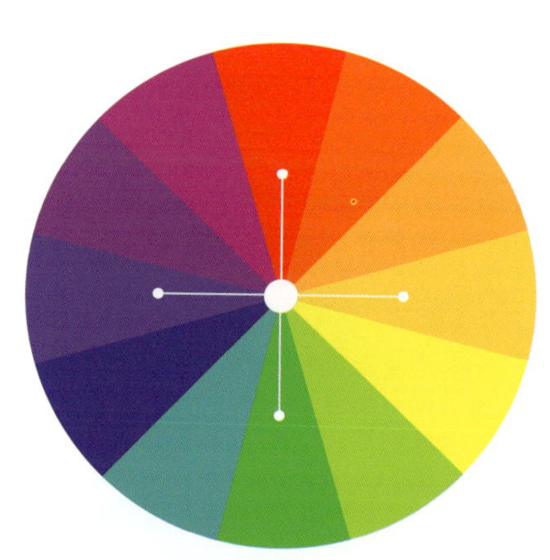

This festive arrangement features a lively *split complementary* color combination of yellow, red-violet and blue-violet. The classic triangular design benefits from the creative addition of curled OASIS™ Aluminum Wire, which breaks the static lines of the mass design and complements the spirit of the composition.

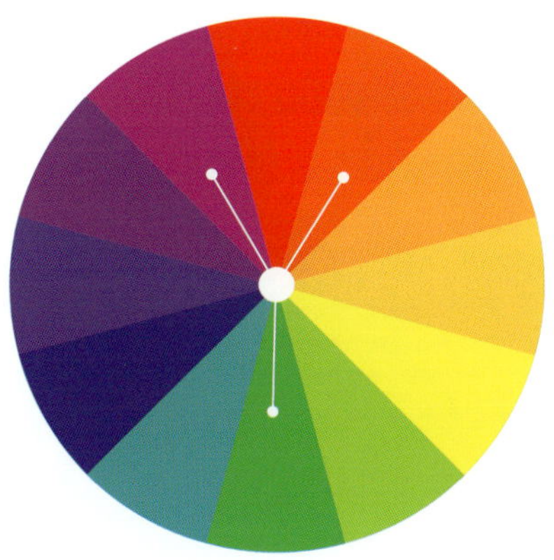

Split Complementary

The *split complementary* color harmony combines three hues: a selected hue on one side of the color wheel and the two hues adjacent to its direct complement. The chosen hues create a "Y" formation in relation to one another on the color wheel.

For example, using yellow as the selected hue, its direct complement is violet, and its split complements are on each side of violet. Thus, the split complementary color harmony would comprise yellow, red-violet and blue-violet.

An arrangement of yellow *Gerbera* with blue-violet *Delphinium* and red-violet *Dendrobium* orchids combine to create a harmonious split complementary color scheme. Split complementary colors may require more effort to combine effectively using fresh flowers, but the results often have a more artistic or exclusive look.

Triadic

A *triadic* color harmony uses three hues that are equidistant from one another on the color wheel. The primary colors of red, yellow and blue and the secondary colors of orange, green and violet are triads. Each of these triadic harmonies are easily created using common cut flowers. Stems of red roses, yellow *Gerbera* and blue *Delphinium* provide a vibrant primary triad. Orange pincushions, green *Anthurium* and violet *Dendrobium* orchids create an exotic secondary triad. The tertiary triads (red-orange/yellow-green/blue-violet and red-violet/yellow-orange/blue-green) require more effort, but variations in color value can help enhance the appeal of these more unusual mixes.

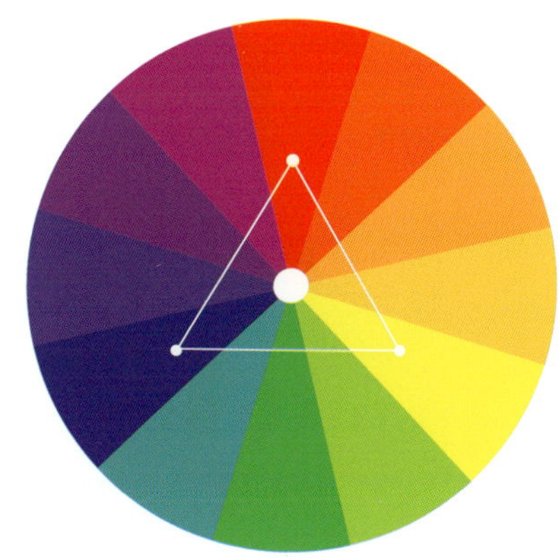

(Triadic continued)
In this triadic color harmony of secondary colors, tints of orange and violet combine with mid-green to create a pleasant bridal look. Violet is the dominant hue, making a statement through three components (carnations, New York *Aster* and ribbon wrap), with stems of peach roses and *Hypericum* and green salal and *Ruscus* providing contrast. Neutral white and silver florals serve to support and unify the color harmony.

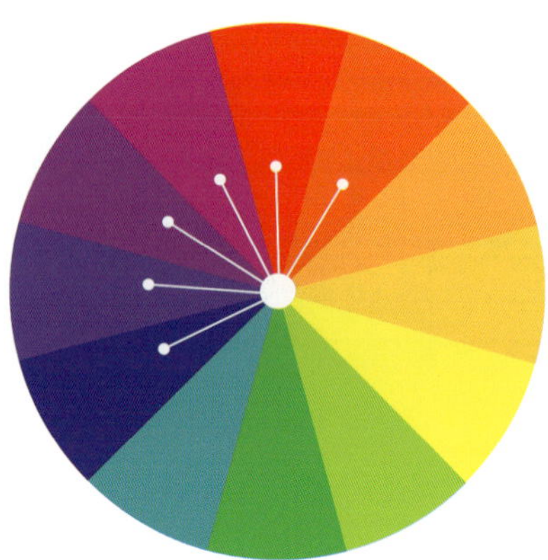

Polychromatic

A *polychromatic* harmony is a discordant color scheme that combines many colors without concern for their relationship on the color wheel. Often, a variety of flower types are used to provide the varied colors; however, it is possible to create a monobotanical arrangement using many colors of one flower type. In either case, it is important to use neutral filler flowers or foliage to help unify the array of colors. Variation can be achieved in a polychromatic design not only by way of the varied hues but also by varying the tints, tones and shades. A polychromatic design made entirely of pastels will have a different impact than one that combines pure hues, deep shades and touches of tints. With so many different colors in one design, it is especially important to develop a strong focal point so the eyes have a defined place to rest.

Red, orange, yellow, green, blue and pink combine to create a vibrant *polychromatic* color harmony in a densely mounded form. Gray *Eucalyptus* and green salal offer a neutral background while *Gerbera* partner to anchor the focal emphasis. While most flowers are used in limited quantity, pink *Boronia* serves as a generously sprinkled filler to unify the broad collection of floral elements.

Additional discordant color harmonies are described in other guides to color. These harmonies involve combinations of four or more colors that may require further study and practice in order to master them. Experimentation is an ideal way to discover flower colors that partner well together.

Consider these tips when working with color:

- Choose one or two dominant colors in a mixed color combination, using less of the other colors in the mix. Equal amounts of multiple colors, or a 50/50 proportion of two colors, weakens the focus of the design.

- Use the warm, advancing colors of red, orange and yellow in lesser amounts when paired with cool, receding colors of green, blue and violet.

- Be thoughtful about the amount and placement of white flowers in a mixed color scheme to avoid diluting the impact of the other colors.

- Balance the placement of colors, using a dominant color in the focal area and transitioning that color, using the same or a different flower type to the edges of the design.

- Use stronger or darker colors, which have more visual weight than light colors, near the base of the design to enhance the visual balance.

- Brighten dark areas of a design with light colored flowers that both extend beyond the design surface and settle deep within the core.

- Repeat some colors using different flower types to avoid the polka-dot effect created when each color in a design is represented by only one flower.

- Draw inspiration for the color scheme of a design from the colors of the container. This will assure a sense of unity between the flowers and the vessel that holds them.

- Use green or silver flowers and foliage as dominant components of a color scheme, or in lesser quantities, as a neutral background element to bridge and connect multicolored designs.

Flowers for Every Color Need

Red		Burgundy/Magenta		Pink	
Alstroemeria	Snapdragon	*Alstroemeria*	*Hypericum*	*Alstroemeria*	*Protea*
Amaryllis	Sweet pea	*Amaranthus*	Kangaroo paw	*Anthurium*	*Ranunculus*
Anemone	Tulip	*Anthurium*	*Leptospermum*	Aster	Rose
Anthurium	*Vanda* orchid	Aster	*Leucadendron*	*Astilbe*	*Scabiosa*
Aranthera orchid	*Zinnia*	*Astilbe*	Lily	*Astrantia*	*Sedum*
Aster		*Astrantia*	*Lisianthus*	Bachelor's button	Snapdragon
Calla		Bachelor's button	*Paphiopedilum* orchid	*Boronia*	Statice
Carnation		*Bouvardia*	Queen Anne's lace	*Bouvardia*	Stock
Crocosmia		Calla	*Ranunculus*	Calla	Sweet pea
Dahlia		Carnation	Rose	*Campanula*	Sweet William
Freesia		*Clematis*	*Sarracenia*	Carnation	Tulip
Gerbera		*Cymbidium* orchid	*Scabiosa*	*Clematis*	*Tweedia*
Gladiolus		*Dahlia*	*Sedum*	*Curcuma*	*Vanda* orchid
Gloriosa		*Freesia*	Snapdragon	*Cymbidium* orchid	*Veronica*
Heliconia		*Gerbera*	Stock	*Dahlia*	Waxflower
Hypericum		Ginger	Sweet pea	*Delphinium*	*Zinnia*
Lily		*Gladiolus*	Sweet William	*Freesia*	
Pincushion		*Gloriosa*		*Genista*	
Protea		*Godetia*		*Gerbera*	
Ranunculus		Heather		Ginger	
Rose		Hyacinth		*Gladiolus*	

Pink	Orange/Peach		Yellow	
Gloriosa	*Alstroemeria*	Hyacinth	*Acacia*	Kangaroo paw
Godetia	Amaryllis	*Hypericum*	*Alstroemeria*	*Leucadendron*
Heather	*Anthurium*	Kangaroo paw	Calla	Lily
Heliconia	Aster	Lily	Carnation	*Lisianthus*
Helleborus	Calla	Marigold	*Chrysanthemum*	Marigold
Hyacinth	Carnation	*Mokara* orchid	*Craspedia*	*Oncidium* orchid
Hydrangea	Chinese lantern	*Ornithogalum*	*Cymbidium* orchid	Pincushion
Hypericum	*Chrysanthemum*	Peony	Daffodil	*Ranunculus*
Kangaroo paw	*Crocosmia*	Pincushion	*Dahlia*	Rose
Leptospermum	*Cymbidium* orchid	*Ranunculus*	Dill	*Sandersonia*
Lily	*Dahlia*	Rose	*Eremurus*	Snapdragon
Lisianthus	*Delphinium*	Snapdragon	*Forsythia*	Statice
Nerine	*Eremurus*	Sweet pea	*Freesia*	Stock
Ornamental kale	*Freesia*	Tulip	*Genista*	Sunflower
Peony	*Genista*	*Vanda* orchid	*Gerbera*	Sweet pea
Pepperberry	*Gerbera*	*Zinnia*	*Gladiolus*	Tulip
Phalaenopsis orchid	*Gladiolus*		*Gloriosa*	Yarrow
	Gloriosa		*Heliconia*	*Zinnia*
	Godetia		Hyacinth	
	Heliconia		*Iris*	

Flowers for Every Color Need

Green		Blue	Purple/Lavender	
Alstroemeria	*Protea*	*Agapanthus*	*Allium*	*Lisianthus*
Amaranthus	Queen Anne's lace	*Ageratum*	*Alstroemeria*	*Mokara* orchid
Anthurium	*Ranunculus*	*Aster*	*Anemone*	Ornamental kale
Artichoke	Rose	Bachelor's button	*Aster* and Aster	*Phlox*
Bells-of-Ireland	*Sarracenia*	*Campanula*	Bachelor's button	*Ranunculus*
Bupleurum	*Scabiosa*	*Clematis*	Calla	Rose
Calla	*Sedum*	*Delphinium*	*Campanula*	*Scabiosa*
Carnation	*Trachelium*	*Eryngium*	Carnation	Statice
Chrysanthemum	*Viburnum*	*Gentiana*	*Chrysanthemum*	Stock
Curcuma	*Zinnia*	Globe thistle	*Clematis*	Sweet pea
Cymbidium orchid		Grape hyacinth	*Dahlia*	Sweet William
Dendrobium orchid		Hyacinth	*Dendrobium* orchid	
Gladiolus		*Hydrangea*	*Freesia*	
Helleborus		*Scabiosa*	Hyacinth	
Hydrangea		Statice	*Hydrangea*	
Hypericum		Sweet pea	Kangaroo paw	
Kangaroo paw		*Tweedia*	Larkspur	
Lisianthus		*Veronica*	*Liatris*	
Paphiopedilum orchid			Lilac	
Poppy pod			*Limonium*	

White/Cream		White/Cream		Black/Brown
Allium	Lily	*Gardenia*	*Veronica*	*Anthurium*
Alstroemeria	Lily-of-the-valley	*Genista*	*Viburnum*	Calla
Amaryllis	*Limonium*	*Gentiana*	Waxflower	Chocolate *Cosmos*
Anemone	*Lisianthus*	*Gerbera*	*Zinnia*	*Cymbidium* orchid
Anthurium	*Lysimachia*	*Gladiolus*		*Dahlia*
Aster and Aster	*Narcissus*	*Gloriosa*		Flax
Astilbe	*Nerine*	*Godetia*		*Heliconia*
Astrantia	Ornamental kale	Heather		*Helleborus*
Baby's breath	Peony	*Helleborus*		Hyacinth
Bachelor's button	*Phalaenopsis* orchid	Hyacinth		*Hypericum*
Bouvardia	*Phlox*	*Hydrangea*		Lily
Calla	*Protea*	*Hypericum*		Peony
Campanula	Queen Anne's lace	*Iris*		Rose
Clematis	*Scabiosa*	Larkspur		Sweet pea
Curcuma	*Sedum*	Sweet pea		
Cymbidium orchid	Snapdragon	Sweet William		
Dahlia	Star-of-Bethlehem	*Trachelium*		
Delphinium	Statice	Tuberose		
Dendrobium orchid	*Stephanotis*	Tulip		
Freesia	Stock	*Tweedia*		

Texture

Texture is both the physical and visual tactile quality of design components. Some flowers are soft or velvety, others are prickly, and some, such as roses, present more than one texture when considering the blossom, the foliage and the stem. Some foliages are smooth, others are bumpy. Some are rough, others are fuzzy. Ribbons may be shiny, satiny or silky, each providing a different impression of its feel. A ceramic vase may have a grainy surface while a bark-covered basket is coarse. Regardless of the physical characteristics of these design components, what matters most is the visual impression they contribute to an arrangement.

Textural variety is a desirable design feature. It adds contrast between design elements and can also serve to unify disparate flower types. Texture enhances visual interest, giving the eyes more to explore throughout an arrangement. It is often the quiet link between unusual flowers and colors and the secret ingredient that enlivens an otherwise ordinary flower mix.

Consider these tips when working with texture:

- Strive for sensible textural proportions. It takes less coarse- or rough-textured material to make an impact than is needed for a soft-textured material to do the same.
- Avoid too many layers of the same texture. A vase of roses enhanced with baby's breath, plumosa fern, *Limonium* and *Astilbe* could become so frothy that the roses are lost in a sea of softness.
- Consider intricate parts of the flowers and foliage that contribute to the textural quality of design materials. Toothed-leaf edges, lash-like stamens, pubescent buds and other unique attributes can be used to enhance visual sensation.
- Avoid textural extremes such as delicate and fluffy fillers combined with bold, coarse focal flowers.
- Recognize the differences in texture that varied flower forms can provide, and strive for diversity. A standard rose and a spray rose, though both velvety, contribute different levels of softness due to their differences in size and delicacy. The same is true when comparing the textures provided by a solid leaf and a dissected leaf or a single mass flower compared to a cluster of tiny blooms.

This mixed flower bouquet offers a variety of textures without notable extremes. *Gerbera* provide a smooth-textured foundation while, by comparison, spiral *Eucalyptus* is visually somewhat coarse, and heather is somewhat soft. Smooth salal leaves provide the most solid form that appears comparatively hard while the tiny seeds of seeded *Eucalyptus* contribute a delicate lightness. The middle textures of *Freesia*, snapdragons and hyacinths, neither highly coarse or soft, provide a cohesive union.

Pattern

Pattern is prevalent among the natural materials used in floral design. The colorful painted effect of a croton leaf provides pattern. The alternating arrangement and descending size of blooms on a stem of *Gladiolus* also forms a pattern. Pattern can be bold or subtle, consistent or random. Consider the difference in pattern between the lively zebra-like markings of a *Calathea* leaf and the understated intermittent banding of *Equisetum*. The variegation and bicoloration common among flowers and foliage provide a plethora of pattern options at a floral designer's disposal.

Pattern is the design inspiration for the Biedermeier design style. By definition, a Biedermeier is made with concentric rings of flowers to create a bulls-eye pattern. In this example, combining rings of a singular flower with others that are patterned (button spray mums with spray carnations, *Stephanotis* with *Hypericum*, *Stephanotis* with *Limonium*) results in a pattern that is defined yet delicate.

The silhouette of a flower arrangement also provides a pattern within which an arrangement is designed. This outline provides a sense of shape and formality. A loose and open design pattern may suggest informality while a tightly defined outline typically appears more formal. The use of space contributes to these differences in pattern and, thus, formality. The manner of positioning flowers in a design can also create pattern. Repetition of a flower type throughout an arrangement provides pattern, particularly when the placements are repeated in a consistent, predictable manner, such as small flowers at the tips and large flowers near the center. Certain design styles, such as a Biedermeier bouquet or a hedgerow arrangement, rely on repeated patterns of flower placements to achieve a recognizable composition.

Consider these tips when working with pattern:

- Make repeated use of line, form, space, color and texture, independently or in combination, to create eye-catching pattern within a design.
- Pair bold patterned materials with unassuming companions to avoid competing interests. For instance, green button spray mums or chartreuse *Bupleurum* provide an unobtrusive backdrop for festive stems of rainbow roses.
- Avoid too many patterns in the same design. "Dress" your flower arrangements with reasonable conservatism, avoiding the look of striped pants, paisley shirt and a polka-dot tie.
- Add pattern to enliven a plain container, a monochromatic color harmony or a monobotanical composition.
- Avoid patterns formed by exact flower placements on each side of center. Allow natural materials the freedom of small variations.

Fragrance

Fragrance is an inherent quality of most natural materials. Some flower fragrances are more pronounced than others, but most have a detectable scent, many of which add desirable qualities to an arrangement beyond the visual. Fragrance preferences are highly personal. The perfume industry exists because of the universal enjoyment of scent and individual preferences for a vast array of fragrances.

When making flower arrangements, the resulting fragrance combination can be coincidental or intentional. Often, flowers are put together without concern for the ways individual scents will meld. But when fragrance is front of mind, flowers can be selected or avoided for the scents they contribute, with the resulting design not only beautiful for the eyes but also a feast for the nose.

Consider these tips when working with fragrance:

- Use fragrance as a design accent, striving to include at least one type of fragrant flower in every arrangement.
- Experiment with fragrance combinations, including sweet, spicy and earthy scents. Consider marketing your fragrance combinations as a floral perfumery.
- Avoid clashes between multiple strong-scented flowers. Consider carefully which companion flowers to combine with powerfully-scented blooms such as lilacs, Oriental lilies, garden roses and hyacinths. Featuring one strong scent instead of several increases the likelihood of a positive response.
- Use pleasant strong-scented flowers to mask the potentially offensive fragrances of common offenders such as *Allium*, boxwood and caspia.
- Avoid unpleasant scents resulting from ripening and decaying flowers and bacterial accumulations in containers by following proper flower care and handling practices.

(Opposite Page)
Row 1: *Freesia*, Lilac, Carnation
Row 2: Rose, *Gardenia*, Stock
Row 3: Oriental lily, Peony, Paper-white *Narcissus*
Row 4: Tuberose, Lily-of-the-valley, *Genista*
Row 5: Sweet pea, Hyacinth, *Stephanotis*

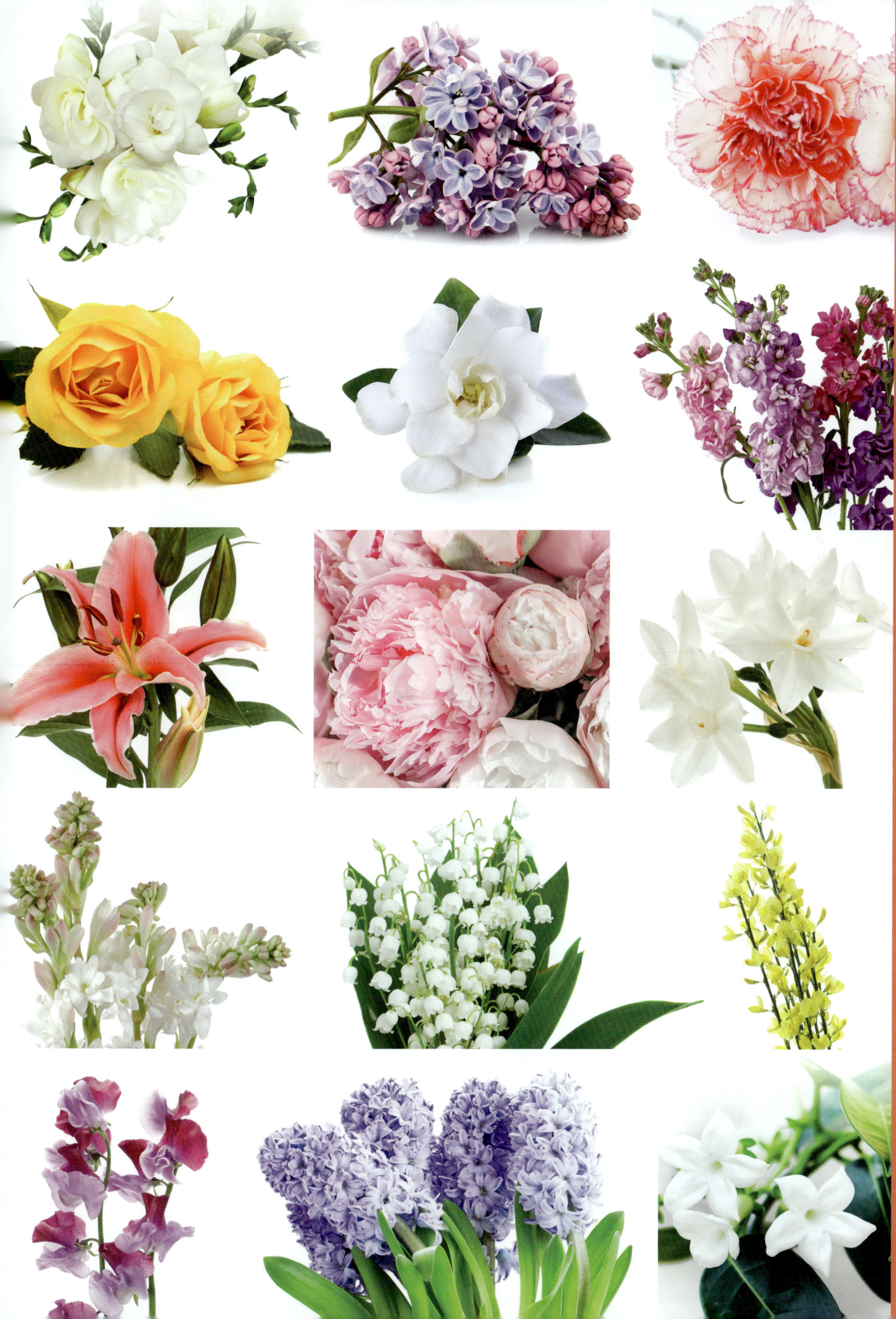

Best Fragrant Flowers For Flower Arranging

GUIDING PRINCIPLES

The principles of floral design are often described as the steps or guides to the creation of successful arrangements. Comparing the design process to a good recipe: the elements of floral design are the "ingredients," and the principles of floral design are the recommended ways of using those ingredients. Sift the flour to achieve a lighter consistency for a delicate cake batter; consider the color or motif of a container to achieve greater unity of an arrangement with its vessel.

A seasoned floral designer follows the principles of floral design instinctively. When watching the work of a floral professional, what may appear as random insertions of stems are actually thoughtful and careful placements positioned with a specific end result in mind. The principles of floral design guide the decision-making involved from the beginning to the end of the design process, including:

- What container to use?
- How tall or wide to make the design?
- What flowers to combine?
- How many of each flower type to use?
- How to prepare the mechanics to support the design?
- Where to place the first flowers?
- How to develop a proper shape?
- How much space to allow around the flowers?
- How to guide the eyes for maximum visual enjoyment?
- How to create focus and hold the viewer's attention?
- How to develop a cohesive color scheme?
- How to use accessories to enhance the design or add a theme?

The principles of floral design are not independent ideals. Their use and effectiveness rely on proper execution of other design principles. Just as the density of an angel-food cake made with properly sifted flour can fall flat if overmixed, good visual balance is not possible if the proportion of the design is too great for the size of the container. Rhythm is lessened in the absence of strong depth. Unity is weakened without smooth transition from the focal area to the design's perimeter.

As you study and master the use of each principle of floral design, consider the impact your choices, placements and techniques have on the other guiding principles. When all of the principles are in sync, exemplary design is achieved, and even untrained eyes will recognize the superior quality of the finished product.

FURTHER READING ABOUT FLORAL DESIGN ELEMENTS AND PRINCIPLES

The elements and principles of floral design are discussed in many floristry publications. Some organize or define them differently, but the overarching teachings are generally quite comparable. This chapter offers a brief introduction to the elements and principles of design. The following books serve as good resources for further reading:

- *The AIFD Guide to Floral Design: Terms, Techniques, and Traditions*
  The American Institute of Floral Designers
- *Principles of Floral Design: An Illustrated Guide*; Pat Diehl Scace, AIFD, and James M. DelPrince, Ph.D., AIFD
- *The Art of Floral Design*, Norah T. Hunter
- *A Fresh Look at Judging*, Hitomi Gilliam, AIFD and Kathy Whalen, AIFD

Balance

Balance is a fundamental principle of floral design. By nature, we find comfort in the sense that objects are anchored, straight or stable. A beverage glass on the verge of tipping creates a feeling of angst. A crooked picture on a wall begs to be straightened. So, too, is the case with flower arrangements.

The principle of balance refers to both the physical and visual distribution of weight in a design. To achieve good physical and visual balance, the proportions of an arrangement to its container are vitally important. An arrangement that is too tall or wide may physically tip and/or may appear on the verge of tipping. Neither is desirable.

Similarly, an arrangement designed too far forward in a container or with the top flowers leaning forward will appear "front heavy". Crookedness, except when used intentionally to create an asymmetrical shape, can also cause imbalance and should be avoided.

Physical balance, also referred to as mechanical balance, relates to the actual stability of an arrangement. A design should be self-supporting. It should be stable on a table, with no need for support. If it is at risk of tipping with a slight brush or bump of the table surface, then it does not have adequate physical balance.

Visual balance refers to the appearance that a design is grounded. It is possible for an arrangement to be physically balanced, with no concern that it will tip over, but still be visually out of balance. Arrangements may be designed with symmetrical or asymmetrical balance. A symmetrically balanced arrangement can be divided into equal halves, thus equal weight. An asymmetrically balanced arrangement has unequal weight distribution when bisected through the center.

Balancing the components of an arrangement is also important. An arrangement made entirely of large flowers in a delicate container may be difficult to physically balance. Large flowers isolated at the top of a design without comparable weight at the base creates undesirable top-heaviness. Placement of large flowers low and near the center of an arrangement helps visually anchor it. Similarly, the placement of coarse foliage or filler should be more centrally located rather than at the perimeter.

When working with asymmetry, it is essential to counterbalance a strong line in one direction with items of similar visual weight on the other side of the design.

Color balance is most easily achieved when a color is equally distributed throughout an arrangement. A greater sense of style results when color is grouped or isolated into limited areas of a design. To balance these colors, consider the relative amount of color in one area compared to another while also taking into account the visual weight each color provides. Pure hues and dark shades are generally heavier than tints and tones. Warm colors read heavier than cool colors.

This asymmetrically balanced arrangement has equal visual weight on each side of center. The even distribution of the green cushion mums combined with the blue *Eryngium* counterbalance the visual weight of the vibrant yellow.

In this one-sided sympathy design, flat fern is positioned near the back edge of the container and is counterbalanced by shorter stems of fern that extend over the front edge. This creates an open silhouette with room for large-stemmed *Gladiolus* to be presented with good posture, thus good balance. Notice the stem count is nearly equivalent on each side of center.

A pair of *Anthurium* anchor the center of this asymmetrically balanced Hogarth curve design. The positioning of bells-of-Ireland in the upper left counterbalances the *Dendrobium* orchids and lily grass in the lower right. Flowers from the violet hue are balanced above and below the green *Anthurium* focal area.

This design exhibits asymmetrical balance inspired by its organic form. Tulips on the left are balanced by orchids on the right while roses anchor the center. The casual juxtaposition of light and bright colors creates an easy sense of equilibrium.

Scale and Proportion

The principles of scale and proportion pertain to size relationships.

Scale refers to the size relationship of an arrangement to its setting. The appropriate size of an arrangement for a church altar will vary depending on whether it is intended for a chapel or a cathedral. To be in scale with the wearer, the size of a boutonnière for a ring bearer should be smaller than that for the groom. A trio of bud vases on a 60-inch round reception table fills the space with better scale than just one. By adding a mirror and votive candles, more space is filled, thus improving the scale of the composite centerpiece. If the reception takes place in a ballroom with high ceilings, a topiary or multitiered design would be an even better option to fill vertical space.

Proportion relates to the size relationships of the design components. An arrangement should appear comfortable in the vessel that holds it. A design that is too large or too small for its container has an equivalent awkwardness of a pair of pants that are too tight or coat sleeves that are too long. A common recommendation is for an arrangement to be 1½ times the height of a tall container or 1½ times the width of a low container. This proportion is in keeping with the Golden Mean, a rule of proportion using a 1:1.5 ratio discovered by ancient Greeks and recognized still as the preeminent guide to artistic size relationships.

Proportion also relates to comparative amounts of design elements used in an arrangement. Generally, a 50-50 relationship between small and large sizes, bold and quiet flower forms, rugged and delicate textures, or advancing and receding colors is not desirable. The more dominant of any of these elements is needed in lesser quantities.

Good color proportion is best achieved when a strong or deep-colored flower is used in lesser quantity than more muted or neutral colors. Effective textural proportion relies on the use of soft textures in larger quantities than heavy textures. An arrangement of orange roses, peach spray carnations and baby's breath should have more peach, less orange; more baby's breath and spray carnations, fewer roses. Following the common rule of thirds, a one-third/two-thirds relationship or similar combination of dominant to subordinate elements provides a good sense of proportion.

Proportion should be considered when combining forms, lines and patterns. Form flowers with unique shapes, markings or other characteristics make an impact in lesser quantities than is needed for mass or filler flowers to do the same. Strong lines and bold patterns can overwhelm a design if used too heavily. The proportion of foliage to flowers is also an important consideration. Too much foliage can diminish the visibility and impact of flowers or require an excessive quantity of flowers relative to the price or perceived value. The number or size of design accessories should also be in good proportion to other design components. A trio of Valentine hearts is better proportioned to a vase of 12 roses than a dozen picks in the same design.

The scale of a wrist corsage should suit the size of the wearer. Here, the proportion of ribbon and gem accessories is suitably subordinate to the flowers.

In this monochromatic monobotanical design, the volume of flowers is well proportioned to the large vase size, and the limited amount of foliage allows the flowers to dominate.

Color is creatively proportioned in this modern design. Lime-colored flowers (*Anthurium* and bells-of-Ireland) are used in greater proportion to the pink spray carnations, providing a dominant to subordinate relationship of about 70 percent to 30 percent. Yet the strong pink colors of the OASIS™ Midollino Sticks and the vase, when combined with the carnations, cause the proportions of the entire composition to shift such that the color pink is approximately 60 percent dominant.

Rhythm

An arrangement is more pleasing to look at when flowers are placed in such a way that the eyes sense a pathway to follow. The term used to describe the visual movement that occurs along this pathway is **rhythm**.

Line is a primary design element used in the establishment of rhythm. Vertical lines draw the eyes up and down, horizontal lines direct the eyes left to right. Diagonal and curved lines can provide endless dashing and sweeping pathways that cause active eye movement. The rhythm of a successful arrangement will cause the eyes to move from areas of dominance to more secondary portions of the design and back again. The focal point of an arrangement should attract a viewer's attention, yet the rhythm should entice the viewer to explore the design in entirety.

The manner in which lines emerge from the container also provides a sense of rhythm. Many classic design styles utilize **radial rhythm**. Also called **radiation**, this rhythm creates visual pathways moving from the center of the container outward in all directions, in a fountain-like fashion. Consider the manner in which fern fronds grow outward in all directions from a common central plant base. The flowers in a radial arrangement should similarly emerge from the center outward. In doing so, stems should not physically or visually cross one another, which can confuse the visual movement. The classic round mound uses radial rhythm, as do any of the triangular design forms. Vase arrangements, hand-tied bouquets and even corsages rely on radial rhythm, as well.

Parallel rhythm is found in some contemporary floral design styles. This parallelism results from the positioning of stems side by side, like trees in a forest. Variations involve parallel stems that are placed horizontally, diagonally or even cascading. The hedgerow design is an example of a style with vertical parallel rhythm. The waterfall design is a style with cascading parallel rhythm. A combination of radial and parallel rhythm in the same design is also possible. For instance, in the vegetative style, like flowers are positioned in natural radiating groupings side by side (parallel) with one another, as if growing in a garden.

Random rhythm is a more advanced manner of artistic arranging in which the visual movement of design elements is less predictable. Often, the space between flowers is made progressively closer together moving from the extremities to the center of an arrangement. This serves to draw the eyes to the area that is most often the focal point. When the placement of flowers and the use of space is irregular, the rhythm is more jarring. This can be an intentional choice of the designer, but if a flowing rhythm is desired, the pattern of flower spacing needs to be consistent.

Rhythm is closely related to the principles of depth, repetition and transition.

The curved and entwined lines of this design create an exciting random rhythm. The intentional crossing lines of the Cloni Pon-Pon *Ranunculus* add complexity to this modern mass design.

Depth

The rhythm of a flower arrangement is increased when the eyes not only move up and down or back and forth but also in and out. **Depth** is the desirable three-dimensional quality of a design. It can be achieved with thoughtful placement of flowers that extend forward beyond the edge of a container, and in one-sided arrangements, by angling the tallest stems slightly backward. This opens the center and prevents the design from looking flat.

A solid surface of flowers is less visually pleasing than a layered design that allows flowers to tuck under and extend beyond the surface. Depth is achieved by varying the lengths of flowers positioned near one another. Those positioned below others may not be entirely seen, but the hints of color and mass that show through the flowers above them are vital to providing a sense that the design is three dimensional. When flowers are positioned at varied depths, the spacing can be opened up and fewer flowers may be needed.

Lilies extend forward at the edge of the container while green *Hydrangea* and carnations tuck in deeper to provide a successful three-dimensional form. *Mokara* orchids and manipulated OASIS™ 3/16" Flat Wire angle both forward and backward to increase the depth of the design.

Repetition

Repetition contributes to the rhythm of an arrangement by providing a recognizable pulse. Repeated use of a color, flower type, line, texture, pattern or other design component provides needed predictability, like the certain beat of a piece of music. Repetition also contributes to a design's sense of unity. An arrangement of a dozen different flowers in a dozen different colors could look like pieces and parts. By adding a filler element and repeating its use throughout the arrangement, what otherwise appears to be a collection of miscellaneous blooms becomes a unified whole. Any repeated element can be the unifying ingredient. Flowers in a color that repeats the hue of the container or lines that repeatedly radiate from the center outward contribute to a design's feeling of compatibility and completeness.

Even in a design as small as a corsage, repetition can be used to enhance rhythm and unity. In this traditional pin-on corsage, every floral element – waxflower, spray roses, *Dendrobium* orchids, micro spray mums and *Hypericum* berries – is repeated from tip to base.

Transition

Transition relates to the manner in which changes occur in a design. These changes may include shifts in size, form, line, color, texture and spacing. Even the direction each flower faces and the transitions among the flower facings should be considered by the designer.

Typically, flower sizes transition from smaller flowers at the perimeter to larger flowers in the center. A natural color transition moves from light flowers at the extremities to darker colors near the center. An ombré design in which flowers from a single hue fade from one extreme to the other, relies on successful transitions between multiple color intensities.

In line-dominated designs, transitions in flower spacing create a more pleasing design than one in which the spacing between all flowers is the same. For these designs, there should be more space between flowers at the tips, transitioning to closer spacing, in some cases even overlapping flowers, near the center. Similarly, flower facings at the tips of an arrangement should look upward or outward while those at the center look forward. The angle or pitch of the stem contributes to the direction a flower faces. Though, generally, smooth transitions are the norm, for some arrangements, the designer may intentionally choose to create a more jarring rhythm by making unexpected transitions that defy norms.

This hedgerow design demonstrates clearly defined transitions between varied flower forms and colors.

The flower colors in this crescent arrangement transition from blue to rose, with greater spacing between the upper *Iris* and the center hyacinths than between the hyacinths and the tulips. The visual connectedness of the spiral *Eucalyptus* on each end creates a smooth transition within the curved line.

In this horizontal centerpiece, the large lily blossoms anchor the focal area, with lily buds and parrot tulips helping to provide size transition between the center and the tips. Flower facings also transition between the forward-facing lilies and the sideward-facing tulips. Lighter colors are emphasized at the tips, with deeper colors used more heavily in the center.

Dominance

Dominance relates to the element of an arrangement that is most impactful. In some arrangements, color makes the most powerful statement. In others, the lines or flower forms dominate. A well-proportioned design will have asymmetry among its components, with some colors, textures, lines or flower forms used in greater amounts than others. Those in greatest quantity are naturally dominant. This is easily demonstrated in an arrangement of a dozen red roses designed with baby's breath and leatherleaf fern. Here, the roses dominate by virtue of not only quantity but also size, form and color.

Red 'Hearts' roses are the dominant element in this woodland topiary. The rich color and velvety texture are more impactful than the subordinate green elements. Their extension beyond the surface of the sphere, with other flowers placed deeper, adds to the attention they command.

Emphasis

Closely related to dominance, the principle of **emphasis** speaks to areas of importance or impact in an arrangement. Many designs have a singular area of emphasis achieved by way of stronger color, closer spacing, greatest energy or other means that bring more attention to a particular section. This is commonly referred to as a *focal area* or *focal point*. Many contemporary arrangements achieve emphasis in multiple areas within an arrangement and sometimes by different means in each area. For example, a parallel systems arrangement may feature *Anthurium* at the top of a system and orchids at the base of one or more systems. The uniqueness of these flower forms and the isolated placement of them create multiple areas of emphasis within the same design.

A trio of parrot tulips with varied flower facings creates the focal area for this cascade bouquet. *Freesia* and micro spray mums nestle deeply into the spaces between them to provide repetition of color and unify the center with the extremities.

Focal Area

Focal area is the term used to describe the most important area of emphasis within a design. It is generally the most interesting area to which a viewer's eyes are instinctively drawn. Traditional radial arrangements typically have a single focal area, most often centered near the base of the container. Sometimes this area is referred to as a focal point or center of interest.

The focal area in asymmetrical styles may be offset in concert with the point where lines of opposition meet. Many contemporary designs have multiple areas of importance, with some more dominant than others. Often, these areas are referred to as primary and secondary points of interest.

A focal area provides a landing point as well as a springboard for the eyes. Here, flowers are typically positioned with the most forward, attention-getting facings. With strong lines and good rhythm, the viewer's eyes will travel along subordinate elements to reach the dominant ones in the focal area. The larger size, stronger color, more-interesting forms or other sources of contrast will hold the eyes and allow them to rest. When all components are working together, the eyes will soon be drawn again to the outer reaches or secondary areas of emphasis.

The term **focal point** may misdirect a designer into thinking a single flower is the key to creating this area of emphasis. In fact, few arrangements other than the Biedermeier style, benefit from this bulls-eye approach. Rather, a collection of flowers unified by relatively close spacing makes a better focal area than a single bloom. To achieve a centered focal area, none of the focal flowers will likely be placed directly in the center. Instead, each should be placed in staggered positions to the left and right of center and above and below center, with facings that shift from upward to outward to downward positions, all with slightly angled profiles rather than projecting directly forward.

Lily stems create multiple points of interest in this sympathy wreath. Their unique forms provide contrast to the collection of round flowers that fill out the wreath base.

Accent

An **accent** is an extra element that gives an arrangement added interest or appeal. Usually, an accent is a unique item that interrupts an otherwise homogeneous blend of ingredients. Yet, an accent should have a recognizable relationship – be it color, theme, style, formality, or occasion – to the other design components.

Ribbon is a common accent, as are occasion-oriented message picks and seasonal accessories. Flowers can also provide accent but only when the chosen bloom type varies notably from the rest of the flower mix and is used in limited quantity.

Usually, an accent is isolated to one area of a design rather than sprinkled throughout it. Resist the temptation to add multiple unrelated accents that can confuse the viewer and divide attention. An accent is typically a planned component of an arrangement, but sometimes the need does not become apparent until a design is nearing completion. A little perspective, achieved by stepping back from an arrangement, often helps the designer analyze and assess the need for such a finishing touch.

Roses are the dominant element in this classic vase arrangement. A satin bow provides a gift-like accent while also marrying the flowers with the container.

Contrast, Opposition and Variation

Contrast, opposition and variation are principles that speak to the strategic use of differences in design elements to make a flower arrangement more interesting. Excessive sameness of color, texture and flower form can make a design appear ordinary or dull. Contrast, and its supporting principles of opposition and variation, provide a means of relieving that boredom.

The principle of **contrast** involves intentional use of dissimilar elements. It is most successful when the contrasts are bold but not brash. Perfectly spherical *Allium* paired with smooth flat *Monstera* leaves provide exciting contrasts of size, texture and form. When the *Allium* are positioned vertically and the *Monstera* is placed horizontally, their contrasts are further emphasized.

Color contrast provides an easily understood example of how contrast can uplift an arrangement. Violet on its own, or paired with blues or pinks, makes a pleasant statement. But when combined with its direct complement, yellow, it instantly gains a greater level of liveliness.

Contrast is often used to achieve emphasis and focal interest. The related principle of **opposition** uses contrasts of polar opposites including size (small/large), color (bold/subdued), texture (soft/coarse), line (static/dynamic), form (filler/focal) and even fragrance (sweet/spicy) to add interest by way of conflict. Tension is an exaggerated form of opposition used to create an intentional artistic rivalry that adds conspicuous drama.

This pavé design offers contrasts in color and texture, as well as contrasts of placements by way of vertical *Equisetum* and lily buds that oppose the flat presentation of round flowers. Crossing lines of *Equisetum* furthers the underlying feeling of opposition.

The principle of **variation** provides a comparatively simpler means of maintaining interest in an arrangement and may result in more subtle, yet effective, differences. Variation is used to ensure similar elements have enough variety among them to be relevant. An arrangement including button spray mums is more interesting when there is size variation provided by buds, partially open flowers and fully developed blooms. A design of round flowers including standard roses and *Ranunculus* is elevated by the branched habit of spray roses. A monochromatic design of pinks provides more to visually explore when the color intensities are varied.

Though contrast, opposition and variation help a designer achieve diversity in design, the skillful designer knows when to dial it back. Variety may be the spice of life, but in flower arranging, there are many situations where less is more.

This modern variation of an inverted-"T" design highlights the dynamic energy that is achieved by opposing colors (orange/green), opposing lines (vertical/horizontal) and opposing flower facings (birds-of-paradise).

Button spray mums in varied sizes, spray carnations placed at varied depths, and daisy spray mums with varied facings provide the variation needed to add interest to a simple round mound design.

Harmony

The components of a flower arrangement, including container, flowers, foliage and accessories, should appear to be in agreement. The colors and textures should look pleasant together. The design as a whole should make sense in its surroundings. When all of those qualities are achieved, a design is said to have **harmony**. A harmonious combination of materials feels right to the viewer. It is easy on the eyes compared to an arrangement with discordant pairings such as exotic tropicals with frilly baby's breath or pastel flowers with a bright red bow.

Generally, extremes are harder to combine harmoniously than materials with something in common. Soft colors make sense with soft textures; bold flowers need a generous container.

Variety is appealing, but if there is no relationship among the mix, harmony will be lacking. Though many exceptions can be made, fail-safe combinations are flowers from the same season, the same growing region or the same hue. The designer should also consider the occasion or setting. Informal flowers such as daisies and goldenrod may not feel harmonious in an opulent ballroom.

Like a musical harmony, the components of a flower arrangement can be elevated when perfectly partnered. Often the solution to an arrangement that doesn't quite sing is the addition of one more flower or filler types to bridge the gap between elements that aren't quite in sync. Still, too much of a good thing can diminish the effectiveness of a design. Orchids, *Anemone*, lily and *Lisianthus* are all lovely flowers, but each has a unique form that may ultimately compete with, rather than complement, the others. Harmony is essentially compatibility, so when in doubt, leave it out.

This waterfall design exhibits a pleasant combination of linear elements to provide the desired cascading effect. A blend of white form, mass and filler flowers comfortably contrast with each other and the lime-green background. Lily grass and curly willow add needed lift and line extension while the gnarled OASIS™ Rustic Wire enhances the nature-inspired harmony.

Unity

Unity is the sense and the appearance that an arrangement is complete, with all components working together to create a satisfying finished product. A unified arrangement has a clearly developed outline, filled in with a well-proportioned flower mix, resulting in a visually balanced three-dimensional form. A unified arrangement has an absence of holes or confusing gaps. Spacing is open enough to showcase the flowers but close enough to visually connect the dots. The arrangement utilizes line to lead the eyes to an area of emphasis where they can rest. In a unified design, harmonious colors and textural variety create interest without becoming busy or distracting from the whole. A unified design features a compatible combination of flower and container styles and colors. Mechanics are stable, minimal and hidden from view.

Unity is achieved through the successful application of the other principles of floral design. When these guiding principles are followed, the elements of design combine to form an arrangement in which its many components feel as one.

A diverse collection of flowers and textures, made cohesive by repetition of color and consistent use of spacing, coordinate with the rosy vase to present a pleasing and unified garden-inspired composition.

Chapter Two

GETTING STARTED

To create a visually pleasing flower arrangement, proper use of the elements and principles of design is essential. To create a design that is structurally sound and capable of sustaining maximum flower life, proper mechanics are the key. A floral designer must engineer a foundation for every arrangement that ensures it is stable and deliverable. The design also must be capable of consistently delivering a solution of clean water and flower food, to support and extend freshness.

This chapter provides suggested methods for preparing containers, providing a source for flower food solution, greening a container and adding accessories. Each design situation has its own set of mechanical requirements – some minimal, others complex – but with a few basic techniques, most arrangements can be prepped and ready to go in minutes. When mechanics are sound, a designer can then enjoy the freedom to focus on creative floral expression.

MIXING FLOWER FOOD

After harvest, flowers and foliages need flower food to keep them fresh. When used properly, these flower foods, such as Floralife, help maintain water movement up the stem and extend flower longevity. Most flower foods have a common formulation, consisting of sugar, citric acid and a biocide. When mixed properly and used consistently, flower food has the capability of improving flower opening and vibrancy while also extending flower life by a few to several days.

When mixing flower food solutions, be sure to use clean containers and warm water, which helps dissolve powdered flower foods. Avoid using metal containers, which can react with the citric acid. Stir well to ensure the solution is properly mixed. To open tight-budded flowers, use a double concentration of flower food until the buds have opened to the degree desired, then move the opened blooms to a flower food solution mixed at the regular rate.

Use properly mixed flower food solution in all storage and design vessels, including buckets, vases, bowls, bouquet holders and water tubes. Soak floral foam in flower food solution, and use the solution instead of plain water when adding to foam-filled containers. Provide customers with flower food packets for home use, and encourage them to follow label directions. When mixed incorrectly, flower food can do more harm than good by providing sugar that can stimulate rapid bacterial growth without enough biocide in a diluted solution to control it.

A multitude of home remedies are offered on the internet as alternatives to commercial flower foods. Always avoid these concoctions in favor of commercial flower foods that have been researched and formulated to provide the proper balance of necessary ingredients. Similarly, advise consumers to follow label directions and avoid home-spun recipes.

WHAT'S IN A FLOWER FOOD?

Flower food, often referred to by the outdated and inaccurate term "floral preservative," contains three primary ingredients, each with a specific role in maintaining flower freshness.

- **Sugar**
  Replaces the flower's natural food source; helps the flower open and develop fully.
- **Acidifier**
  Typically, citric acid; reduces pH, improving water uptake.
- **Biocide**
  Reduces the growth of harmful micro-organisms that cause stem blockage.

SOAKING FLORAL FOAM

Floral foam, such as OASIS™, provides a long-lasting water source for flowers. In fact, flowers arranged in OASIS® Floral Foam Maxlife have been proven to last as long or longer than flowers designed in a vase or other direct water source. To achieve these results, floral foam must be soaked properly.

Fill a deep sink, bucket or tub with properly mixed flower food solution to a depth greater than the height of a brick of floral foam. Drop the block on top of the solution, and allow it to float freely as it takes up the solution. A standard brick of OASIS® Floral Foam Maxlife measures nine inches by four inches by three inches and holds about two quarts of solution.

As the foam absorbs the solution, it will slowly sink until the top of the brick meets the top of the water, where it will continue to float until it is removed. Full saturation of a floral foam brick takes up to two minutes.

***NOTE:** Never force floral foam under water to hasten water absorption. Doing so will result in the development of air pockets inside the brick; flower stems inserted into these dry areas of the foam will have no water source.*

Cutting Floral Foam

Floral foam should be cut to a size that fits comfortably inside the container. OASIS® Floral Foam Maxlife bricks are scored at increments of one-half and one-third. Many standard floral containers hold exactly one-half or one-third of a brick. An easy way to estimate the foam required is to lightly press the base of the selected container into the top of a foam brick, making an imprint.

For many applications, it is desirable for the foam to extend about one half-inch above the lip of a small container or as much as an inch above the lip of a large one. This allows for easy insertion of horizontal stem placements. If the foam is not tall enough to rise above the lip, a slice of foam in the bottom of the container can serve as a riser under the larger foam block. Some modern design styles require a more flush base, in which case the foam may be applied at or below the container edge.

When the floral foam fills nearly every bit of the container, it is necessary to create a water well. By notching a deep opening in one edge of the floral foam, usually at the back of the intended design, flower food solution can be added as needed so the floral foam provides the flowers with a continuous supply of flower food solution.

Beveling the edges of the floral foam provides more easily accessible surface area for angled stem insertions. This is accomplished using a floral knife to slice off all corners and ninety-degree angles.

Vertical containers require a slightly different approach. A floral foam brick turned on end and trimmed to fit the entire depth of the container is one option. Alternatively, foam scraps can be placed in the lower portion of the container to support a solid block of foam in the top half or third. In either case, the flower food solution be replenished often so the top block of floral foam is in contact with the solution. It is not advisable to wedge a block of foam into the top of a container without support beneath it because this creates the possibility that the foam will dislodge and fall to the bottom.

Securing Floral Foam

Floral foam should be secured into containers to prevent shifting during the design process and mishaps during delivery. Several options are available to secure the foam depending on the type of container and the intended design styling.

OASIS® Waterproof Tape, available in quarter-inch and half-inch widths, is typically crisscrossed over the foam and adhered to the edges of the container. Though waterproof tape is highly adhesive to most surfaces, occasionally, it needs reinforcement. In this case, a short piece of waterproof tape can be applied horizontally at the edge of the container across the end of the tape that spans the top.

Baskets typically have plastic liners into which the floral foam can be glued or taped. Securing the liner into the basket, however, requires a different approach because glue will seep through the basket weave, and waterproof tape does not always adhere well to wicker. A thick rubber band provides a handy solution. Simply stretch the band over the basket handle and slide it down to the base of the handle. The taut band will secure the liner and is easily hidden among the flowers.

Hot glue provides a convenient alternative to taping floral foam in place. Either a glue gun with **OASIS® All-temperature Glue Sticks** or a glue pan with **OASIS® Hot-melt Glue** pillows can be used to adhere dry floral foam into a container. Cut the foam to fit the container, apply the glue to the base of the foam block and press it into place. A glue pan provides quick even coverage and speeds the process when filling several containers at one time. Once the glue is set, usually in less than a minute, the entire container, with attached foam, can be submerged in a tub of flower food solution to soak.

PROPER USE OF FLORAL FOAM

Floral foam allows a designer to create arrangements of nearly any imaginable shape or style. It provides a water source to sustain fresh flower life, but only when flowers are properly inserted. It is essential for every flower to be inserted deeply into the wet foam. Flowers that are inserted less than an inch or more into the foam may be unstable. They may easily fall out of position, especially as more flowers are added or when the design is moved for wrapping, delivery, etc.

When a designer inserts a flower deep into a design and then decides it needs to be positioned higher, it is essential to remove the flower and make a new insertion in a different spot. Simply making an adjustment by pulling the flower up slightly in the same hole will damage the necessary stem-to-foam contact that assures the flower will receive its supply of flower food solution.

When a designer makes multiple adjustments in the same arrangement, removing flowers and reinserting into new holes, the integrity of the floral foam can become compromised. Too many vacant holes creates a "Swiss cheese" effect that can result in complete collapse of the foundation. To prevent this fatal error, hold stems near their intended placement before cutting, measuring the needed length, and then inserting with confidence.

OASIS™ Anchor Pins are another possible mechanic for securing floral foam. These four-pronged plastic holders, reminiscent of the implement that keeps the cheese off the inside lid of a pizza box, can be secured, prongs pointed upward, with hot glue, florist clay (**Floralife® SURE-STIK® Floral Adhesive**) or **OASIS® UGLU™ Adhesive** to containers of many types. They are used singly to hold a small piece of foam or in multiples to hold larger pieces. The cut foam is simply pressed onto the prongs, and no taping is required.

Using Chicken Wire

Some flower arrangements, especially large sympathy designs or altar arrangements, benefit from added support for tall and thick-stemmed flowers. Chicken wire (OASIS™ Florist Netting) is a helpful aid that provides a secure grid atop the floral foam to prevent stems from collapsing or breaking the foundation.

Using an **OASIS® Designer Urn**, cut a piece of green **OASIS™ Florist Netting** to a size slightly larger than the container opening. Fill the urn with soaked floral foam, standing a full brick on end in the center of the container and wedging small pieces of foam around it. Apply the OASIS™ Florist Netting across the top of the foam, and tuck the ends inside the edges of the container. Use two straps of waterproof tape to secure the foam and OASIS™ Florist Netting in place.

Preparing Vases

Vase arrangements suit today's consumer preferences for natural-looking bouquets. There are multiple ways to prepare the mechanics for these types of designs. The simplest is to fill the vase with flower food solution and begin adding flowers. Often, however, a stabilizing foundation is preferred to help hold flowers in the desired positions both during and after the design process.

Floral foam is sometimes used to achieve desired looks in vases and cubes. When the container is clear, the foam must be hidden. This can be achieved by adding decorative elements, such as ribbon or floral wraps to the exterior of the container or by lining the interior with fresh foliage. In this example, the floral foam is cut with room to spare so that foliage can be slid into position. The base of each salal leaf is clipped to provide a flat surface that rests comfortably at the bottom of the cube. Overlapping leaves disguise the foam on all sides, including leaves that are strategically folded to fill the corners.

A **grid** is a useful vase support that divides the mouth of the container into smaller openings. Ready-made grids, usually made of white or clear plastic, are available from floral product suppliers in an assortment of sizes to fit over the tops of standard-sized vases. Alternatively, **OASIS® Waterproof Tape** or **OASIS® Clear Tape** can be strapped in two directions to achieve a similar custom-made grid. This allows the designer to determine the preferred number and size of openings atop the vase. OASIS™ Florist Netting (chicken wire) can similarly be trimmed and taped over the top of a large vase to create a sturdy grid.

Decorative marbles, pebbles or gravel in the bottom of a vase also provide stability when flower stems are inserted deeply into this weighted base. Usually, an inch or two is enough to add support. Use caution when adding the marbles to a glass container: Tip the vase on an angle and gently slide the marbles in to prevent breaking the vase.

Greening Containers

The process of preparing a container with foliage prior to arranging the flowers is commonly referred to as "greening" or "greening up." Typically accomplished with one to three types of foliage, greening a container before arranging the flowers serves several purposes: It establishes the basic outline or silhouette of the arrangement, it diffuses the appearance of flower stems, it provides transition between the container and flowers, it covers mechanics and it provides a background to showcase the blooms.

Generally, the foliage framework created when greening up traditional arrangements should be slightly smaller than the finished design will be. This does not preclude the use of accent greens in ways that extend beyond the flowers, but it helps assure that the flowers are the emphasis of the design. Some modern arrangements feature foliage used quite minimally or as only an accent. For those designs, other methods, such as collaring or mossing, replace the initial greening process.

Traditional Greening for One-sided Arrangements

Leatherleaf fern is a staple of the floral industry, providing a deep green color and a lacy texture, as well as reliably long vase life at an affordable price. It is the standard foliage for greening arrangements. Here, it is used to demonstrate the process for greening a one-sided arrangement in a triangular shape. This process can be modified for other one-sided design shapes by changing stem lengths and positions.

Cut a stem of leatherleaf fern approximately 1.5 times the height of an upright container, and center it near the back of the foam. Pitch the stem on a slight angle backward as you insert it. Trim two pieces of fern about half the length of the first and insert them on each side of the container against the rim. These stems should be positioned with upward facings.

Cut two more pieces of leatherleaf to a length slightly shorter than the pair on the sides. Insert these stems at the front edge of the container so that they create a "V" formation, with both stems radiating from near the center of the foam, extending forward but away from each other. Cut two additional pieces of fern about half the length of the tallest centered stem, and insert them on each side of center, angling from the center outward.

Add three to six additional fern tips radiating from the center outward, covering the remaining visible foam. Turn the container around, and add a few small pieces of fern to cover the foam in back.

Traditional Greening for All-around Arrangements

All-around arrangements are designed to be viewed from all sides. Greening up an all-around design requires even distribution of foliage and a balanced overall shape. From a birds-eye view, the outline should be clearly circular, creating a perfect template for the addition of flowers.

Prepare a container with floral foam, and secure with waterproof tape. Avoid crossing the tape directly in the center. Begin greening using pieces of leatherleaf fern that extend horizontally to a similar length at the container edge.

Overlap the pieces of leatherleaf to create a continuous circular outline. Use a slight downward angle so the finished collar of greens arches slightly downward, creating a union with the container.

Position three larger pieces of leatherleaf vertically in the center of the container, with each stem arching outward in a different direction from the others. These fronds should essentially face one another like friends gathered at a party.

Cut leatherleaf into segments to create tip and base pieces of varied sizes, and use them to fill in the foam between the greens at the top and edge. With proper radiation, the resulting green foundation should look like a small fern plant.

Lacing

Arrangements made without floral foam involve a different manner of greening up. Lacing is a technique involving creating a network of interwoven stems that support and hold each other in position. The more stems that are added, the more interlocked and supportive they become. Whether designing in an open-mouthed vase through a grid or in a narrow cylinder, lacing helps create a foliage foundation that supports flower placements. It is also the process used without a vase to make hand-tied bouquets.

Prepare a vase with flower food solution and a base of marbles, if desired. Add six stems of leatherleaf fern positioned around the edge of the vase as horizontally as the stems will allow. Stems should cross diagonally through the vase from one side to the other, with stems ending at or near the bottom.

Add three stems of leatherleaf, inserting them through the other greens so they stand somewhat upright in the center. The natural arch of the leatherleaf will provide a graceful radial rhythm from the center outward.

Add three to five stems of leatherleaf between the top three stems and the six at the edge, following the same radial pattern from the center outward. As these stems are added, the laced network should solidify, creating a stable foundation for the addition of flowers.

Mossing

Mossing is a manner of container preparation in which moss is utilized to camouflage the floral foam in place of (or sometimes in addition to) foliage. Sheet moss or Spanish moss are typically used to cover the foam and mechanics.

When using sheet moss, soak it first, and then squeeze out any excess water. Next, pull the moss gently to create a loose-knit layer. When using Spanish moss, which is typically used dry, a thin layer is best. If either type of moss is applied too thick, it may be necessary to pierce the moss with a knife in order to insert stems through it. Greening pins or short pieces of florist wire bent into hairpins should be used, as needed, to secure the moss in place.

Collaring

Collaring is a basic greening technique sometimes used for round arrangements, centerpieces and bouquets. It involves creating a ring of greens around the edge of the container only, leaving the center open for flowers. Often this is done with broad-leaf foliages such as **Galax**, ***salal or*** **Magnolia**, ***but any type of foliage, from feathery plumosa fern to spiky*** **Equisetum** ***to graceful bear grass, can be used, depending on the look desired.***

This technique is especially effective for design styles in which the flower placements are very dense, creating a thick mass of flowers over the uncovered foam.

In this collaring variation, stems of 'Green Trick' *Dianthus*, arranged around a basket edge with close spacing, provides the impression of fresh moss.

Adding Accessories *(Pages 58-61)*

Accessories are added to many arrangements to create a theme, add personality or inject a bit of whimsy or humor. Some accessories, such as candles, serve a function; others partner a keepsake gift together with the blooms. Often, accessories serve as a design accent, providing contrast and interest to the focal area or a secondary area of emphasis.

Some of the simplest accessories are decorative picks shaped like butterflies, birthday cakes, baby rattles and other symbols of seasons, holidays and life events. These are simply poked in place, often at the top of the design or in a central opening between flowers. Other accessories include plush animals, ceramic figures, fruit and candy.

Attachment methods vary greatly depending on the type of accessory and the desired placement in the design. Keepsakes must be handled with care, avoiding glues or other adhesives that might leave a sticky residue. Plush animals need a water barrier to prevent wicking water from the wet foam. Although many accessories require one-of-a kind mechanics, the techniques on Pages 58-61 are widely used.

Candle Mechanics

When adding candles to a flower arrangement, a designer must assume they will be lit by the recipient. Wicks should be trimmed to one-eighth to one-quarter inch to ensure a clean burn. Flowers should be no more than one-third the candle height in the area immediately surrounding it. Wispy fillers, such as Limonium *and bear grass, should be avoided near the candles to prevent the possibility of ignition.*

Sometimes, taper candles are inserted directly into the floral foam. This basic mechanic is acceptable if the candle is inserted deeply enough, generally to the point at which it firmly resists pressure. A lasso of waterproof tape, starting on one edge of the container, wrapping around the candle base and then continuing to the other side of the container, provides added security.

Candleholders provide an alternative means of securing tapers. These plastic adapters have a cup to hold the candle and a stake for insertion into the foam. Similar candle stakes are available for pillar candles, or wireless wood picks can be used instead. Simply wrap the pillar base with half-inch-wide waterproof tape, then apply a single pick and wrap again, repeating with three more picks to create a four-legged base ready for insertion into the floral foam.

Occasionally, a candle is too thick or too thin to fit into a candleholder. If the candle is too thick, shave the base with a floral knife to fit the holder. If the candle is too thin, use waterproof tape wrapped several times around the candle base until the required thickness is achieved.

Anchor pins are an effective mechanic to secure votive cups into arrangements. Use hot-melt glue, florist clay or adhesive dashes to secure the base of a votive cup to the top of an anchor pin. Insert the four prongs of the anchor pin into the floral foam until the top of the anchor pin rests atop the foam.

Mechanics for Plush Items

When a plush animal, doll or other fabric-based accessory is placed in a flower arrangement, it must be secured in a manner that does not mar the item in any way. Rather than gluing, taping or piercing devices onto or into the plush item, the preferred mechanic involves using ribbon or chenille stems to add wood picks, which can then be inserted in the floral foam.

Twist a chenille stem around an arm and another around a leg of a plush animal.

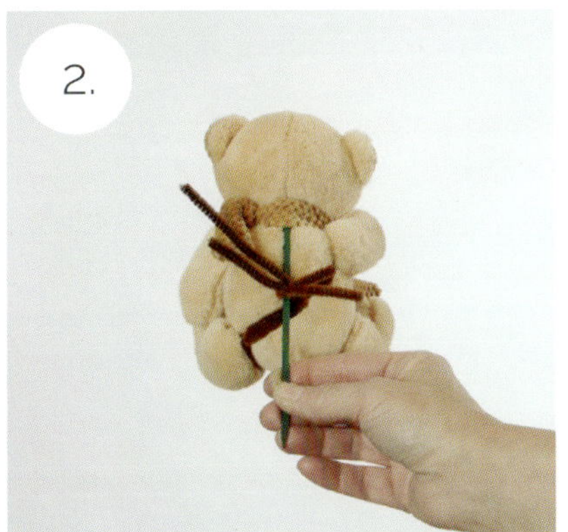

Twist the ends of the two chenille stems together behind the animal. Then twist the chenille stems around an wireless wood pick. Trim the ends of the chenille stems, or tuck them so they are hidden.

Trim a boutonnière bag or flower wrapper to create a piece of plastic or cellophane slightly larger than the base of the plush item. Place the plastic on the surface of the floral foam, then insert the wood pick through the plastic so the plush item rests comfortably on top of the plastic water barrier.

Mechanics for Ceramic Figures

Ceramic figurines are a common feature in holiday arrangements and sympathy designs. Many can be attached using the same chenille-stem-and-wood-pick method described above for plush items. When the ceramic figure has a hole in the base, an alternative picking method can be used.

Insert two wireless wood picks (or two hyacinth stakes for taller ceramics) into the floral foam, in the area where the ceramic figure is desired. Angle the picks away from each other, forming a "V."

Push the tops of the wood picks close enough together to fit inside the hole in the bottom of the ceramic figure. Position the ceramic over the picks, and lower it onto them, releasing the pressure on the picks.

As the ceramic figure is slid into place, the wood picks will return to their outward-angled positions, providing pressure inside the ceramic and holding it firmly in place.

Mechanics for Succulents and Special Flowers

Fresh design elements with short or no stems sometimes require special mechanics. To place a stemless succulent into an arrangement, insert a wireless wood pick into the base of the succulent, adding OASIS® Floral Adhesive, as needed, to secure the pick.

Different pick sizes will suit smaller and larger succulents. If the pick can be inserted deeply enough, adhesive is not necessary to hold the pick in place. In this case, the succulent will be a viable plant once the arrangement has perished, so the use of glue should be avoided. Simply set the rosette on top of a pot of soil in a sunny window, and water occasionally. The succulent will eventually develop roots and anchor itself in place.

Short-stemmed specialty flowers, such as *Cymbidium* orchids, sometimes need support in order to use them singly in a design. Here, a wood pick is taped to the stem, leaving the stem end uncovered so it has the benefit of a water source once inserted into floral foam.

Mechanics for Edibles

Edible accessories may be used in flower arrangements in two ways: as a gift to be consumed by the recipient and as a decorative design element not intended for consumption. Candy is a common edible intended for consumption. Boxed candy and candy bars can be picked using hot glue or adhesive dashes or strips on the exterior of the wrapper, with the picks inserted into the desired position in the design.

Loose candies are best bagged with cellophane, tulle or a boutonnière bag, then tied with ribbon. A wired wood pick twisted around the cinched bag provides a mechanism for insertion into the design.

Fruits and vegetables make effective natural design accents. Seasonal combinations include pumpkins and gourds, apples and pears, bananas and kiwis, or carrots and radishes. Some produce, such as asparagus and celery can be inserted directly into the floral foam, just like stems of flowers. Others, such as grape clusters, require attachment to a wired wood pick.

Many rounded fruits and vegetables, including apples, oranges, peaches, plums, eggplants, mushrooms and Brussels sprouts, can be prepared with wireless wood picks inserted into the flesh. The larger and heavier the produce, the more likely a pair of picks will be needed. Insert these picks so they angle away from each other. This creates a solid insertion that will not spin in the foam base.

Fruits and vegetables used in flower arrangements often attract positive attention. Due to the dye on the wood picks, which will seep into the flesh of the produce, a care tag should be attached to the arrangement cautioning the recipient to not eat the produce.

Chapter Three

ALL-OCCASION DESIGNS

Flowers have long been used as a means to convey messages, express emotions and enhance settings. Life events are a primary motivator for flower purchases. From birthdays, anniversaries and new babies to graduations, retirements and engagements, flowers elevate occasions to something more special. Flowers help people say thank you, I'm sorry and get well soon. They also create ambiance whether it be a romantic dinner for two or a celebratory banquet for 200.

To meet the floral requirements of these and other occasions, a designer needs a storehouse of design options. Many of the classic design styles are based on geometric shapes while modern styles may be inspired by nature, architecture, art or other influences. In this chapter, we present representative samples of all-occasion design styles including classic and modern. Step-by-step instructions provide a systematic approach to each design that can be adapted to different situations, containers and flower combinations. Thoughtful application of the principles of floral design throughout the design process will help to ensure pleasing results.

SYMMETRICAL TRIANGLE

SUGGESTED MATERIALS:

- Larkspur
- Standard Carnations
- Cremone (Disbud) Chrysanthemums
- Micro Spray (Pompon) Chrysanthemums
- Statice
- *Hypericum*
- Myrtle
- Leatherleaf Fern

The symmetrical triangle is a shape with many applications in flower arranging. Its symmetry provides a sense of order and formality. When all sides of a triangle are the same length, the result is an equilateral triangle. Arrangements designed in this mass design shape often appear grand or stately. The isosceles triangle, which is characterized by two sides of the same length, is typically designed as a tall and narrow arrangement. Its upright posture is similarly dignified but with less-imposing mass, making it a highly versatile one-sided style. Here we demonstrate the process for designing an equilateral triangle.

DESIGN STEPS

Prepare an oblong container with soaked floral foam, securing the foam in place with waterproof tape. Be sure the foam extends at least one-half inch above the container's edge.

Use a single stem of linear myrtle to establish a central line extending to a height approximately one-and-a-half times the width plus height of the container. Insert this stem near the back center of the foam, then add two shorter varied length stems on each side of center. Position these stems so they angle slightly from the center outward. Add a stem of myrtle extending horizontally from each side of the foam. The measurement from the tip of one stem to the tip of the other should be equal, or nearly so, to the height of the tallest upright stem of myrtle. Partner a second shorter stem of myrtle with each side placement.

Extend several stems of myrtle two to three inches beyond the front container edge with a slight downward angle to buffer the connection of the arrangement with the container. Add linear stems of myrtle on each side of the central line to develop the triangular framework.

Use additional stems of myrtle in the center of the container to complete the three dimensional form. Vary the stem lengths, and angle them so they radiate from the center outward.

Fill in the spaces between the myrtle with tips of leatherleaf fern. Be sure the floral foam is well hidden by the greens. Use a few pieces of leatherleaf to cover the foam in back.

Use a stem of larkspur to extend the central line slightly beyond the myrtle. Partner two additional stems of larkspur on each side of center, at shorter staggered heights. Place one stem of larkspur on each side of the container to extend horizontally, slightly beyond the myrtle. The measurement from one tip to another, both side to side and side to top, should be equal.

Cut the tips from two stems of larkspur, and use them to create a "V" extending forward at the front edge of the container. The remaining colorful portion of each of the two larkspur stems should be positioned between the top and the side points of the triangle. Add larkspur buds to help fill out the triangular silhouette.

Create a staggered line of standard carnations from the tip to the base, leaving space in the center for focal flowers. The facings of the flowers should shift as they progress from the top to the base so that the top carnations face skyward and the lowest flowers face forward.

Place a trio of cremone chrysanthemums in a zigzag pattern to complete the central line. Vary the facings of these flowers similarly to those of the carnations.

Add carnations to fill the spaces between the central line and the established sides of the triangle. These flowers should face somewhat sideways. Avoid crowding too many flowers into the gaps so there is space remaining for fillers.

Starting near the top, add a stem of micro spray chrysanthemums in the space between the carnations. Keep the mums intact, using a single stem to position the cluster. Stagger additional micro spray mums on each side of center, then add statice in a similar fashion, tucking some of the statice in deeper than the surface flowers.

Add *Hypericum* berries to fill in gaps and further unify the design elements. Some stems can be cut into two segments, allowing for variety of size among the berry clusters.

A matching pair of scalene triangles, each with sides of three different lengths, make a stylish statement suitable for a church altar, head table or extended buffet. When designing mirror-image designs, consider making both simultaneously for most consistent duplication.

In this isosceles triangle, tall *Delphinium* are used to maximize proportions in relation to the container. This helps create sides that are longer than the base of the triangle. *Grevillea* foliage and *Delphinium* buds are used sparingly to define the sides, allowing plenty of open space, which keeps the design light. Primary colors transition from blue at the tip to red in the focal area, with yellow button spray mums serving as the connecting element.

This asymmetrical design has a strong right angle that is rooted in the triangular form, but the negative space between the snapdragons on top and the horizontal *Delphinium* on the right create a silhouette with a distinctive "L" shape. Contrasting magenta daisy spray mums provide strength in the focal area while green wheat and button spray mums add a flared counterbalance on the left.

VERTICAL VARIATIONS

Vertical arrangements are simple variations of triangular styles. By stretching the height to maximum reasonable proportion and shortening the base of the triangle to little more than the container width, attention shifts from mass to line with extra emphasis on the focal area. Creative use of negative space reduces the quantity of flowers needed, proving that big impact can be achieved with a few dramatic flowers and a powerful linear rhythm, as shown on the opposite page.

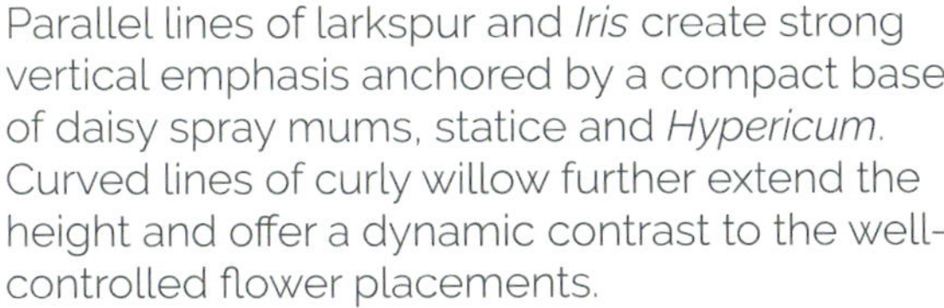
Parallel lines of larkspur and *Iris* create strong vertical emphasis anchored by a compact base of daisy spray mums, statice and *Hypericum*. Curved lines of curly willow further extend the height and offer a dynamic contrast to the well-controlled flower placements.

Curly willow and bells-of-Ireland curve left and right in tandem to create a gentle rhythm that contrasts with the straight stem and flared flowers emerging from the birds-of-paradise. *Gerbera* daisies hold attention at the base while purple statice and stock blossoms, tucked in deep, complete the secondary triadic color harmony.

ROUND MOUND

The classic round mound is an all-around design style with a circular base and domed top. Radial rhythm is fully realized in this mass design because the flowers are positioned so they appear to emerge from the center outward in all directions. The mounded form can be made densely spaced or open and airy. It is the centerpiece of choice for round banquet tables or any situation where the arrangement will be viewed from all sides.

When making a round mound, it is important to visualize the desired shape, extending flowers so the sides are rounded. Deep insertions add dimension, drawing the eyes into the center and adding visual weight to the core. Focal emphasis can be achieved by changes in flower size near the center or by use of more dramatic flowers in key locations, but by virtue of its all-around form, this style may not have any particular focal point. Even distribution of color, texture and flower types helps develop a sense of unity among the design components.

SUGGESTED MATERIALS:

Daisy Spray (Pompon) Mums

Button Spray (Pompon) Mums

Spray (Miniature) Carnations

Limonium

Leatherleaf Fern

DESIGN STEPS

Prepare a container with soaked floral foam, then green up the container with leatherleaf fern following the steps for "Traditional Greening for All-around Arrangements" in Chapter 2.

Cut the stems of three daisy spray mums to a length one and one-half times the height of an upright container. Position the mums in the center of the foam, with slight angles away from each other, to form three points of a triangle above the greens.

Position three daisy spray mums horizontally at the edge of the container, with equidistant spacing. The stem lengths should be equal to and consistent with the length of the horizontal greens.

Add one or two daisy spray mums in each of the spaces between the first three edge placements to complete the circular outline of flowers. All of the edge flowers should be similar in length and positioned like spokes on a wheel.

Visualize a curved line connecting the top flowers to the edge flowers, and position a daisy spray mum in the midsection of the arrangement so the bloom extends to a length that meets the envisioned curve. Rotate the container and repeat this step two more times.

Cut three daisy spray mums to a length one to two inches shorter than the previous three mum stems, and position them in the midsection of the arrangement between the flower placements from step 5. These flowers should sit closer to the foam, creating depth.

Add about six to nine additional daisy spray mums so they are evenly distributed throughout the round form. Follow a similar manner of positioning flowers at the surface and closer to the foam as described in steps 5 and 6.

Add spray carnations in the spaces between the daisy mums, beginning on one side of the arrangement and working from base to top. Place some spray carnations at the surface and others closer to the foam.

Proceed around the container to evenly distribute spray carnations on all sides. Use blooms of varied sizes including buds to provide needed variety.

Add button spray mums in the remaining gaps beginning on one side of the arrangement and working from base to top. Extend these flowers slightly beyond the surface created by the mums and carnations.

Proceed around the container to evenly distribute button mums on all sides. Use a few shorter stems to add depth.

Add *Limonium* with radiating stem placements to extend tips beyond the flower surface. Distribute the filler evenly to fill gaps and unify all design components.

This round arrangement features a broad mix of flower types in a domed silhouette. Form and focal flowers, including roses, *Alstroemeria* and *Mokara* orchids provide contrast and add interest among the mass flower forms of *Ranunculus*, *Gerbera*, spray carnations and daisy mums. A variety of textural filler flowers enhance the combination.

The large flowers and loose structure of this round mound create an easy, carefree spirit. Apricot peonies and rosy pink lilies form the central mass, while snapdragons, sword fern, *Pittosporum* and plumosa fern fill the gaps and extend organically beyond the mound.

Anthurium and spider *Gerbera* combine in this bold circular mass design. The square wood container provides the perfect contrast of circle and square. Salal and *Eucalyptus* provide a quiet background while globular *Craspedia* playfully define the perimeter of the rounded silhouette.

The low spreading profile of this round mound variation demonstrates an alternative silhouette within the same rounded form. Classic Biedermeier styling is achieved using concentric rings of flowers and colors, with textural filler elements adding variety and interest.

OBLONG CENTERPIECE

The oblong centerpiece is the classic arrangement for situations that call for a long and low design. The horizontal emphasis suits an oval or rectangular dining table or coffee table. It also provides a suitable base for a unity candle and looks at home on a bridal head table. As a holiday table centerpiece for Thanksgiving, Christmas or Easter, vertical interest might be added in the form of one or more taper candles, but generally, the form of the oblong centerpiece relies on horizontal placements with radial rhythm.

When choosing materials for an oblong design, consider one or more linear materials such as larkspur, *Delphinium*, spiral *Eucalyptus* or myrtle to establish the outline; a large flower type for focal emphasis; and midsize flowers for transition from tips to center. When using spray (pompon) chrysanthemums or spray (miniature) carnations, incorporate a variety of flower sizes from bud to fully open blossoms. Avoid using large or multi-blooming flowers such as standard carnations or *Alstroemeria* at the tips. The key is to develop a tapered shape, with volume in the center and lightness at the perimeter.

SUGGESTED MATERIALS:

- Lilies
- Tulips
- Snapdragons
- Stock
- *Hypericum*
- Sword Fern
- Leatherleaf Fern
- Spiral *Eucalyptus*

DESIGN STEPS

1.

Prepare an oblong utility container with soaked floral foam. Insert a pair of 15-inch taper candles deep into the center of the foam, allowing at least one inch between them. If the candles are placed too close together, the heat from the flames will cause them to burn and melt faster. Secure the floral foam into the container with waterproof tape.

2.

Extend a stem of sword fern from each end of the foam, angling it downward so the tip is in contact with the tabletop. The length of each of these stems should be equal to, but no longer than, the length of the container. Add slightly shorter stems of sword fern on each side of the initial placements, radiating outward. Extend two shorter stems of sword fern from each side of the foam in a "V" formation, with the tips touching the tabletop.

3.

Add sword fern at the edge of the container between the "V" and the tips. Ensure the length of these stems contributes to a smooth oval outline. Add two pieces of sword fern of similar length on each side of the tapers, extending slightly upward and toward the ends of the design.

4.

Use leatherleaf fern to complete the green up and hide the remaining visible foam. Begin by placing tips of leatherleaf in the middle of each "V," and continue to the top of the foam, keeping the greens low and spreading so the candles remain prominent.

Follow the same general pattern of insertions to add spiral *Eucalyptus* in a symmetrical radiating pattern throughout the established framework.

Place three snapdragons into each end of the foam in a manner similar to the sword fern in step 2. Allow some of the snapdragons to lift away from the tabletop with a comparable arch to the *Eucalyptus*. Place two additional snapdragons on each side of center, angling them similarly but more broadly than the "V" formation of the sword fern in step 2.

Place two stocks in each end of the design, with stems slightly shorter than the snapdragons. Repeat in the center of each side of the design. Use an additional stem of stock (for a total of 10 stems) on each side of the candles, with strong angles toward the elongated tips.

Position two stems of open lilies on each side of the design, at the base of the candles. Distribute any lily buds on angles toward the perimeter.

9.

Distribute *Hypericum* berries throughout the core of the arrangement, placing the most heavily berried stems closest to center.

10.

Accent the design with tulips, pairing them together in any remaining gaps. The finished design silhouette should arc from one tip across the center to the opposite tip. Flowers should meld with the table and completely conceal the utility container.

This oblong centerpiece is designed with asymmetrical balance, providing a short end and clear directional rhythm toward a long end. Focal emphasis is positioned slightly off center to the left, with color transitioning from red-violet at the center to blue-violet at the tips.

Asymmetrical placements of *Grevillea* foliage extend freely in this nature-inspired variation of the oblong centerpiece. The core of the design delivers a symmetrical and whimsical mass of textural elements that appear to be plucked from the roadside. Curls of OASIS™ Rustic Wire, some wrapped in yarn, unite the center and enhance the neutral palette.

SUGGESTED MATERIALS:

Roses
Spray Roses
Tulips
Cymbidium Orchid Spray
Dendrobium Orchids
Stock
Anemone
Scabiosa
Lisianthus/Eustoma
Dianthus
Button Spray (Pompon) Mums
Hypericum
Echeveria
Dusty Miller
Seeded *Eucalyptus*
Variegated *Pittosporum*
Salal

FREE-FORM CENTERPIECE

The ever-expanding array of "garden" flowers available in today's floral marketplace has increased the desire for free-form design shapes. Geometric outlines are giving way to looser, more organic silhouettes with interesting asymmetrical balance and multiple points of interest. These designs may appear to bend or break the laws of nature inherent in the principles and elements of design. Yet, careful consideration and creative interpretation of line, form, color, texture, balance, proportion, rhythm and harmony is essential to a successful result. In fact, all of the principles of design are important in these arrangements. The trick is to apply the principles in such a way that the design appears effortless.

Here, a free-form centerpiece is designed to suit both round and rectangular or oblong table shapes. Flowers are allowed to extend freely, both horizontally and diagonally. Vertical lines are avoided to reduce any sense of formality or stiffness. Points of interest on every side of the design are different, with limited repetition of flower types. The result is casual and graceful, allowing the flowers to pose as they please.

DESIGN STEPS

Shape a piece of OASIS™ Florist Netting (chicken wire) to form an open sphere that fits neatly inside a compote. Be sure the height of the sphere rises an inch or so above the top of the container. Use twists of OASIS™ Florist Wire or OASIS™ Bind Wire, or the ends of the chicken wire itself to secure the ball formation. Add flower food solution to the container.

Insert stems of broad-leaf foliage intermittently around the edge of the bowl to create a partial collar. Stems should be inserted through the chicken wire and extend deep into the container. Here, a mix of variegated *Pittosporum*, dusty miller and salal are used to provide variety and asymmetry.

Complete the collar by adding a finer textured foliage in the remaining spaces around the perimeter. Seeded *Eucalyptus* is used in this example to comfortably drape over the edges. Using a dramatic flower, such as a stem of *Cymbidium* orchids, extend a line diagonally from the center to one side of the design.

Add a different form/focal flower, such as tulip, to create a diagonal line in the opposite direction. Visualize the diagonal line continuing through the center and out the other side, and position a *Dendrobium* orchid or similar line flower in that position. Use tulips to create a shorter horizontal line in the opposite direction across the center. Anchor the center with a mass flower such as 'Green Trick' *Dianthus* positioned directly atop the chicken-wire foundation.

Use stock and spray roses to establish the center, varying stem lengths and angles while maintaining a semirounded core. Maintain open spacing between these placements.

Use clusters of button spray mums or similar mass flowers placed close to the chicken wire to fill the biggest gaps and provide depth. Add staggered placements of *Lisianthus*, with generous spacing in between. Accent with *Hypericum* berries and single-blooming *Dianthus* to expand the mix of flower forms.

Anchor the top of the rounded core with a pair of upward-facing roses. Then, add a single rose with a more angled facing on each side of the design, leaving a gap between these roses and the centered pair. Insert a wood pick into the base of an *Echeveria* or other succulent, and tuck it in the gap between the roses. Repeat with a second *Echeveria* on the other side.

Unify the perimeter with the core by positioning a few form flowers in the spaces between the initial diagonal and horizontal flowers. Here, a single *Anemone* and a few casual *Scabiosa* complete the loosely structured centerpiece. Though seventeen different botanicals are combined, the design conveys a cohesive sense of style.

This upright variation of the free-form centerpiece utilizes similar horizontal and diagonal placements, with added curvature provided by the arching stems of tulips and callas. A single stem of ornamental kale anchors the core while eclectic groupings of *Acacia*, carnations, *Hypericum*, *Grevillea* foliage and foxtail fern supplement the primary placements. In place of chicken wire, the clear glass container features a foundation of polished stones and a supportive armature formed from a network of submerged curly willow stems. A bound grouping of *Scabiosa* pods provides a distinctive diagonal accent while a single stem of *Nandina* creates a canopy that shelters the stylish flowers below.

TOPIARY

SUGGESTED MATERIALS:

- Roses
- Carnations
- Button Spray (Pompon) Chrysanthemums
- Poppy Pods
- Salal
- Silver Dollar *Eucalyptus*
- Plumosa Fern
- Strong, Straight Branches
- Sheet Moss
- OASIS™ Bind Wire
- OASIS® Waterproof Tape
- OASIS™ Greening Pins
- 6" OASIS® Floral Foam Sphere
- OASIS® Floral Foam Maxlife
- Ceramic or Weighted Container

Topiary, as a floral design style, draws its inspiration from the artistic horticultural practice of trimming or training trees and shrubs into geometric forms or other creative shapes. The classic standard topiary features a single stem or trunk with a spherical top. Variations include multi-stemmed or stem-less foundations and conical, spiraled or multi-sphere tops.

Topiary bases must be heavily weighted to balance the inherent top-heaviness of the designs. Sometimes, the weight of soaked floral foam is sufficient. Stones, sand or gravel added to the container can add more weight. Several techniques can be used to establish topiary mechanics, the easiest of which is to use an OASIS® Floral Foam Sphere or an OASIS® Floral Foam Cone to create the desired style. Alternatively, floral foam can be carved to suit, with chicken wire layered over the foam for added structure and stem security.

To achieve the geometric forms typical of most topiaries, the flowers must be closely placed. Often, the flowers form an even surface, with less depth than a typical flower arrangement. Still, some degree of variation in the depth of primary and secondary flowers helps maintain the integrity of individual blossoms. The base of a floral topiary can be finished with greens, moss or other decorative elements. When flowers are added to the base, the materials should coordinate with those above in order to unify the top and bottom into a complete whole.

DESIGN STEPS

Bundle three strong straight branches, and secure with OASIS™ Bind Wire about two to three inches from the top and the bottom of the stems. Wrap several times, making sure the wire is tightly bound, then twist the ends to secure.

Fill a ceramic or weighted container with soaked floral foam so the foam spans from edge to edge. The foam must be tight within the container to ensure the stem will be stable under the weight of the top. Insert the bundle of stems deeply into the center of the foam until it cannot reasonably be inserted further.

Secure the floral foam and the stem by wrapping waterproof tape from the edge of the container around the stems to the opposite side of the container. Repeat this lasso wrap in the opposite direction so the foam and the stem are doubly secured.

Impale a soaked floral foam sphere onto the top of the bundled branches until it resists pressure, centering the sphere while pushing it into place. Secure the sphere using waterproof tape as follows:

a. Wrap the tape around the bound stems so it overlaps itself.

b. Continuing with the same piece of tape, wrap up and over the sphere and down the opposite side.

c. Still using the same piece of tape, wrap around the stems, overlapping the original tape wrap.

d. Rotate the topiary a quarter turn, and wrap up and over the sphere and down the opposite side so the sphere is secured from all directions.

Lightly green the sphere with salal tips, followed by silver dollar *Eucalyptus*. Keep the greens close to the foam, and avoid unnecessarily covering the entire sphere. When fully greened, about half of the foam should still be visible.

Add plumosa fern, allowing the tips to extend one to two inches beyond the other greens. When complete, about 40 percent of the sphere will still be visible.

Using 12 roses, cut the stems to about 1½ inches, and insert them so that the base of each flower rests against the foam. Here, 'Hearts' roses are used in a fully open stage to maximize coverage. Place the roses with facings in all directions – upward, outward and downward – with flowers used singly and in pairs.

Fill in the largest gaps between the roses with about 18-22 standard carnations. Insert the carnations about one half-inch deeper than the roses, again facing them in all directions so a globular form is developed.

Add individual button mums singly and in groups of two and three in the gaps between the flowers. Extend the mums to a height between that of the roses and the carnations. Intersperse poppy pods lightly throughout the sphere to provide added texture and interest.

Cover the foam base with damp sheet moss, using greening pins to secure it in place. Allow some of the moss to extend slightly over the container edge to cover the ends of the waterproof tape.

Add a simple rose and carnation accent at the base, including salal for contrast and to unify the base with the top. The finished topiary should appear as a fully formed globe with a comfortable sense of balance and physical stability.

Stems of carnations bound into a close-knit unit provide the rounded top reminiscent of a topiary in this frilly variation that uses the natural stems of the flowers to form the topiary "trunk." Start by assembling about a dozen fully open carnations in the hand, raising the center-most blooms to achieve a mounded form. Secure the unit near the grip with clear OASIS™ BIND-IT™ Tape, then insert the stems as a unit into the foam base. Add ribbon to cover the tape, then design a low round mound of filler and accent flowers. For a more open topiary form, try this technique using bundled *Alstroemeria*, spray roses or *Solidago*.

'Free Spirit' roses and *Leucospermum* anchor this densely populated topiary designed using a LOMEY® Column to form a clear "stem" connecting the rounded top with the cozy mounded base. Flower forms and colors pleasantly contrast in this eclectic lime, peach and tangerine collection of Asiatic lilies, *Ranunculus*, miniature *Gerbera*, *Viburnum*, *Hypericum*, button spray mums and *Bupleurum*. A free-flowing vine cascades from the top and encircles the base, softening and unifying the design components.

This pair of petite topiaries draws inspiration from the mushroom world, relying on squatty proportions and spreading tops to make casual and whimsical statements. Both are designed in three-inch OASIS® Floral Foam spheres atop random bundled stems. The tin containers and simple bases add to the informality.

Left: *Gerbera* daisies with a collar of huckleberry form an umbrella-like top over a dense base of 'Green Trick' *Dianthus*.

Right: Hot pink and ivory miniature *Gerbera* combine with *Hypericum* berries, waxflower and plumosa fern to form a nearly globular mound. A mossy base with simple foliage treatment is dressed up with a spirited spin of aluminum wire, providing a harmonious union with the metal container.

VASE ARRANGEMENTS

Vase arrangements are an enduring design style that never really goes out of fashion. Whether large or small, one-sided or all-around, mixed or monobotanical, they have become the preferred look or style among both professionals and hobbyists. Mechanics for constructing these arrangements vary, but most designers agree that once one is proficient with the design process, vases are faster and easier to make than most other styles.

Though often made of glass, containers for vase arrangements may be tin, ceramic, plastic, resin, or any number of other materials, sometimes requiring liners, but always filled with flower food solution to keep the water clean and extend flower life. Vases with a cinched top are easier to design in than those with a wide mouth. Beginning designers may find that a grid across the top of the container helps support flower placements that otherwise fall easily out of position. A substantial green up with a network of crossed stems can significantly improve stability. Using a clear vase can assist in the learning process because stem angles and lengths are visible.

ONE DOZEN ROSES

The quintessential vase arrangement is the dozen rose bouquet. The formula is consistent: twelve flowers, a couple different greens, filler for texture and a bow. The shape, typically circular at the edge and mounded over the top, should showcase every flower. The simplicity of the design is deceiving, and beginning designers may find it challenging to achieve the desired shape due to irregular stem lengths or loose placements that shift during the design process. By trimming all stems to a similar length and building a stable base of greens, these issues can be overcome, yielding a uniform and secure finished composition.

Fill a vase with flower food solution to within a few inches of the top, and add decorative marbles to create a one- to two-inch layer. Follow the steps for "Lacing" in the "Greening Containers" section of Chapter 2 to establish a foundation of leatherleaf fern. To this base, add six or seven stems of Israeli *Ruscus*, allowing it to rise above the fern. Then add seven to nine stems of plumosa fern at a height midway between the leatherleaf and the *Ruscus*, radiating the greens from the center outward in all directions.

Prepare the roses by removing any petals that are damaged or falling away from the head. Consider removing rose thorns if they are so large or dense that they inhibit insertion into the network of greens. NOTE: Take care to avoid damaging or stripping the "bark" on the stems; remove only the tips of the thorns, if possible.

Add a supportive splint wire to any weak-stemmed rose by inserting the end of a No. 20 gauge wire into the base of the bloom and gently wrapping the wire along the length of the flower stem. A gentle wrap rather than a tight spiral makes the wire relatively inconspicuous.

Trim three roses to a height approximately one-and-one-half times the height of the vase. Insert the three flowers through the network of greens, and position them in the center of the vase so the trio forms a triangle. Be sure the ends of the rose stems are pushed among the marbles in the base for security.

Trim five roses to a common length slightly shorter than the first three stems. Insert each of these flowers diagonally into the vase, with the stem ends inserted near the edge of the container. These flowers should form an even circular outline two steps below the triangular trio, leaving a gap between these blooms and the top trio.

Trim the four remaining roses to a common length similar to the edge flowers, and arrange them in the space between the three roses at the top and the five around the edge. These blooms should be angled slightly away from center, with consistent space between them at this midlevel of the design.

Fluff stems of baby's breath so the blooms are separated, and insert them at a height just below the rose heads. Begin at the top of the vase, and progress to the edge of the design, just below the bottom ring of rose stems. Allow occasional breaks between the tufts of baby's breath, providing breathing room within the design.

Create a multiloop bow with streamers using No. 9 ribbon. Secure the bow with florist wire, and attach it to a wood pick before inserting it at the lip of the vase. Trim and shape the streamers as desired.

MIXED FLOWER VASE VARIATIONS

Mixed flowers, including linear larkspur, give this stately vase design a pointed-oval silhouette. Leatherleaf fern and green Pittosporum *provide a solid foundation to support the polychromatic combination of roses, carnations, stocks, larkspur and button spray mums. Multiple filler flowers, including statice, waxflower, seeded* Eucalyptus *and* Grevillea *add texture and variety. A simple ribbon tie around the neck of the vase repeats the purple hue of the statice and larkspur, and enhances the unity of the vase with the flowers. By choosing a variety of flowers and colors, spacing them so all are showcased, and extending the height to maximum recommended proportions, consumer perception of the design's value is increased.*

Design by Heather Bauder

This casual mixed vase design offers a relaxed asymmetry due to the arching edge placements of snapdragons, *Boronia* and plumosa fern as well as the off-center extension of *Eucalyptus parvula*. Clever repetition of color and flower forms, including coral spider *Gerbera* and peonies; rosy spider *Gerbera* and lilies; and yellow lilies, button spray mums and *Freesia*, creates a sense of unity despite the singularity of many of the floral components. A variety of fillers – waxflower, *Solidago*, *Limonium*, myrtle and *Craspedia* - each used lightly, provides an abundance of texture that enhances the free spirit of the design.

DECORATIVE VASE TREATMENTS

Today's exciting array of floral accessories provides many creative options for enhancing vase arrangements. Whether enlivening the exterior of a vase, the interior, or both, decorative accents can upgrade a container while adding personality and value. Use these examples, featuring OASIS® Floral Products, as inspiration for imaginative custom vase treatments.

A: Spin Apple Green OASIS™ Aluminum Wire around the waistline of a Gathering Vase from Smithers-Oasis, bending it to provide a repeated ripple.

B: Carefully pour an inch or two of marbles into the bottom of a Paragon Vase from Smithers-Oasis, and add a Double Row Square-Stone Wristlet around the cinched neck.

C: Thread individual blue beads (clipped from OASIS™ MEGA Beaded Wire) at random throughout a length of Blue OASIS™ Aluminum Wire. Coil the wire creating an irregular pattern, leaving a free end several inches in length. Place the wire coil into a Taper Square Vase from Smithers-Oasis, extending the free end over the edge, wrapping and looping it randomly around the exterior. Secure the end of the wire over the lip of the container.

D: Secure a strip of Pear Leaf OASIS™ Natural Wrap around a Gathering Vase from Smithers-Oasis with OASIS® UGLU™ Adhesive Dashes. Add a tight triple wrap of Gold Matte OASIS™ Etched Wire, using jewelry pliers to secure the ends with a twist in back.

ONE-HALF DOZEN ROSES

When designing a half dozen roses in a vase, typically the goal is to maximize the impact of the six flowers. A one-sided design is a good choice, to assure that every flower is featured. Here, huckleberry, salal and Pittosporum *combine to provide a broad background of greens, with roses staggered in two rows, each row forming an inverted "V."* Limonium *extends beyond the flowers to expand the design size, and a loosely formed bow of two-inch Eggplant OASIS™ Raw Jute adds a nicely proportioned accent.*

BUD VASES

The bud-vase design is one of the simplest compositions, yet potentially every element of design is incorporated within it, and every principle of design must be considered when making it. A bud vase is essentially a small vase, usually narrow, sometimes tall, and most often with a relatively small opening that will accommodate a single blossom or a small collection of flowers and greens.

Good proportion is vital to successful bud vase design. A design that is too short will appear squatty while a design that stretches beyond the 1.5:1 to 2:1 desirable ratio of flowers to container will appear unstable. Large flowers used too high in a bud-vase design will create a top heavy appearance. Too much width can also create uncomfortable weights and proportions. With so few flowers, focal emphasis is usually easily achieved, yet the strategic use of secondary flowers or fillers is important to achieving a sense of unity and harmony among the limited components.

The classic single rose bud vase presents the flower above the container, at a height similar to, or slightly taller than, the vase. In this example, myrtle provides the extension needed for the design as a whole to achieve proper proportion. Salal and *Pittosporum* add needed volume to anchor the base while *Limonium* offers texture and a No. 3 multiloop bow provides a harmonious accent.

The staggered placements of this three-flowered bud-vase variation demonstrate the importance of rhythm to draw the eyes from the base to the tip and back again. Notice, also, the changes in flower facings from the top rose, which appears to look upward compared to the other two roses, which are positioned with facings to the left and right.

BUD VASES FOR ALL SEASONS

This collection of bud vases demonstrates several possible variations in size, shape and flower combination, each with a nod to a particular season of the year.

A. Spring
Vibrant tulips, *Freesia* and *Anemone* form a simple clutch of flowers that appear dropped in a Elite Bud Vase from Smithers-Oasis. *Eucalyptus parvula* fills the gaps, and a few wraps of beaded wire create a decorative collar.

B. Summer
A single sunflower anchors this vertical combination of *Delphinium*, *Aster* 'Monte Cassino' and *Eryngium*. Aloe OASIS™ Raw Jute provides a simple band connecting the flowers to the Cylinder Bud Vase from Smithers-Oasis.

C. Autumn
A classic stair-stepped combination of cushion *Gerbera*, *Solidago* and statice in a Sabrina Bud Vase from Smithers-Oasis achieves a well-spaced and balanced design. Fresh wheat, mahogany *Galax* leaves and an accent of trimmed Corn Husk OASIS™ Natural Wrap complete the feeling of fall.

D. Winter
Branches, *Hypericum* berries and evergreens combine with *Alstroemeria* and spray carnations in this holiday-inspired winter mix. The wide-mouthed Pineapple Vase from Smithers-Oasis readily accommodates the volume of stems and is enhanced by Copper Matte OASIS™ Sequin Wrap.

CUBE ARRANGEMENTS

Bridging the gap between bud vases and vase arrangements are the popular cube arrangements. Cubes can be designed with or without floral foam. If the cube is clear, floral foam can be hidden by various wraps on the exterior or by fresh elements on the interior. Cubes provide a great way to showcase a few interesting blossoms or an eclectic mix of short-stemmed leftovers. Often, these are designed in low mounded shapes, which are easy to deliver and display.

(A) A four-inch cube is lined with a red ti leaf to hide the floral foam that supports this complementary combination of lime green and rich red. Roses anchor the center while *Hydrangea*, cushion spray mums and *Anthurium* round out the form and tips of New Zealand flax provide a diagonal flare.

(B) A trio of *Echeveria* fill a three-inch cube enrobed in Natural OASIS™ Raw Jute wrap and enhanced with binding of Copper Matte OASIS™ Etched Wire and spirals of Copper OASIS™ Aluminum Wire.

(C) A five-inch cube takes on a tropical vibe with a base of *Hydrangea* and fuji mums complemented by *Gerbera*, *Mokara* orchids and birds-of-paradise. See Chapter 2 for instructions for the foliage container lining.

SUGGESTED MATERIALS:

Anthurium

Miniature *Hydrangea*

Bells-of-Ireland

Spray (Miniature) Carnations

Lily Grass

VASE ARMATURE

An armature is a decorative mechanic. It provides a creative means of supporting flower placements or controlling their positions while contributing added color, texture or contrast and enhancing interest. Armatures are frameworks typically crafted from fresh and permanent materials, including branches, reeds, cane, OASIS™ Midollino Sticks, grasses, leaves, raffia, yarn, decorative wire, OASIS™ Bind Wire, copper tubing, etc. Often, an armature adds a sculptural element that artistically elevates a design. Here, an armature is used in the creation of a vase arrangement with a dominant horizontal line that would be difficult to achieve without the supporting mechanic of OASIS™ Midollino Sticks.

DESIGN STEPS

Align eight to ten OASIS™ Midollino Sticks into a bundle, and secure each end with OASIS™ Bind Wire, wrapping three to four times before twisting the ends of the Bind Wire together. Cut about ten Midollino Sticks in half. Clip several two-inch pieces of Bind Wire, and set aside.

Spread the Midollino Sticks apart, in the middle of the bound unit and use the half sticks to create random crossbars, threading over and under multiple sticks in the bound unit so the crossbars hold in place. As needed, twist clipped pieces of Bind Wire around the Midollino Sticks to secure the intersections between pieces.

Continue adding Midollino Sticks to develop a complex, crisscrossed network. Add Bind Wire, as needed, for stability.

Align five or six full-length Midollino Sticks, and bind one end of this unit to one end of the original unit that became the base for the crisscrossed network. Repeat with a second unit of five or six sticks on the opposite end of the base. Holding the network of Midollino Sticks horizontally, gather the free ends of the two newly bound units, and gather them to form a handle below the Midollino Stick network. Add four to six half sticks to the handle, and bind at the grip. Bind the tops of the half sticks to the network of sticks, thus strengthening the center.

Trim the handle of the armature to a length that allows the horizontal framework to rest against the lip of the vase. Place the armature in the vase, and add flower food solution. Insert three *Anthurium* through the armature so the flowers are spaced equally apart, with stems one to two inches above the armature.

Add two or three stems of miniature *Hydrangea* to fill in the gaps between the *Anthurium*. The *Hydrangea* blooms should rest at a level just below the *Anthurium*.

Add a long stem of bells-of-Ireland to the vase. Carefully bend the stem, and coax it through the armature toward one end to reinforce the horizontal line. Use Bind Wire, if needed, to secure the position. Repeat on the opposite end with a second stem of bells-of-Ireland. Add spray carnations through the center and extending horizontally toward the tips, using the armature to support their positions and binding as needed.

Add eight to ten blades of lily grass, inserting stems into the vase, then threading them through the armature to control their directional flow and maintain the horizontal emphasis.

DESIGNS INSPIRED BY NATURE

In contrast to the classic design styles that are derived from geometric shapes, nature has inspired a collection of modern design styles that replicate the way plants grow. Each of these styles presents the flowers as a slice of the natural landscape. Traditional radial stem placement, flowing from a central point outward, is combined with parallel stem placement, essentially lining up vertical floral materials side by side as they might grow along a fence or in a meadow. The influence of the designer should not be evident.

In these designs, foliage is used more thoughtfully as a contributing design element than as a background. Greening up is minimal or skipped altogether, with moss being a common finishing element used to hide mechanics. In classic design styles, effort is made to present the flowers with varied forward facings. In nature-inspired arrangements, the flowers ignore the viewer to some degree, as they do in nature, facing forward, sideways and even backward. Upward flower facings are also prevalent, replicating the way flowers in nature seek the sunlight.

Several contemporary design techniques allow a designer to achieve desired realism in these natural styles:

GROUPING

Isolating different flower types to their own areas of an arrangement. Stems are positioned so that the forms of the individual flowers are featured. It's the opposite of "salt and peppering" flower types together in traditional mixed designs.

BASING

Creating a decorative foundation of materials from which the feature flowers extend. Often highly detailed and textural, basing provides a sense of stability or grounding. In nature-inspired designs, basing mimics the layer of earth from which plants grow.

Paving (Pavé)

A basing technique in which flowers of the same type are positioned close together in a low mass or continuous pathway that may be all one height or may rise and fall within a low profile. The term *pavé* is French for "pavement," "cobblestone" and "paving stone" and comes from the jewelry industry where it is used to describe rings, pendants or other jewelry that is pavéd with multiple gemstones positioned very close together. The pavé technique can also stand alone as a design style.

CLUSTERING

Similar to the grouping technique but with less space among the grouped flowers, fillers or greens, resulting in a close-knit cluster that emphasizes texture or color more than individual flowers.

Pillowing

A variation of clustering using rounded or puffy flowers, such as carnations, *Trachelium* or 'Green Trick' *Dianthus*, to form low mounded "hills" at the base of the container, often with dips between pillowed clusters, providing the appearance of hills and valleys..

Tufting

A variation of clustering typically using linear or plume-like filler materials, such as heather, *Solidago*, *Thryptomene calycina* or *Astilbe*, with several stems of similar length grouped into a tight cluster so that the tips burst forth in a radial manner. Tufting is most often used as a basing technique but also can be a design style (referred to as a "tuftwork design") when numerous tufts of different flower types are positioned side by side to create the desired form, most often round.

TERRACING

The positioning of floral materials to provide the look of horizontal layers, often with space in between, forming a stairstepped appearance. Terracing can be implemented close to an arrangement's foundation, where it is considered a basing technique, or it can occur among flower groupings at all levels of an arrangement, such as a hedgerow design.

ZONING

A technique involving the organization of floral materials into distinct zones, typically using groupings of flower types (or colors) in different areas of the design, with notable variation in height or position among groups placed vertically or horizontally or both.

SHELTERING

A method of placing floral materials or other decorative elements, such as lily grass, OASIS™ Midollino Sticks or OASIS™ Aluminum Wire, in a protective position over other elements of the design so that the flowers below the shelter are at least partially visible. Sheltering often involves creating a canopy above a design or a caged effect over the focal area.

Veiling

A sheltering technique utilizing sheer or filmy floral material (e.g., plumosa fern or sprengeri fern) or other fine design elements (e.g., sheer ribbon or OASIS™ Bullion Wire) layered above or directly on top of other design elements so that the viewer peers through the veil to see the design beneath it. Veiling is most commonly used in the waterfall design style.

FRAMING

The strategic placement of curved or angled branches, greens or flowers on one or both sides of a design, aligned like parentheses, so that attention is held inside the frame they provide.

VEGETATIVE DESIGN

The vegetative style is a nature-inspired style depicting a segment of a landscape such as a garden or a meadow. It is characterized by flower groupings that follow the natural growth patterns of the plants they depict. Authenticity of seasons, climates and native habitats contribute to the realism of this design style, meaning the designer should avoid combining flowers that bloom in the spring with flowers that bloom in the summer, or flowers that grow in a bog with flowers that grow in the desert, and so on.

This vegetative design is depictive of a dense thicket, featuring Queen Anne's lace together with bracelet honey myrtle and *Acacia* foliage in a loosely formed silhouette. Accents of yellow *Craspedia* enhance the vertical interest while the upright log appears as a decaying tree trunk, its rich color and rugged texture dominating the center of the composition and anchoring the base.

This vegetative variation provides a singular statement using multiple containers. Here a garden of tall, medium and short flowers is portrayed using radial stem placements within parallel groupings. Negative space is used strategically to separate groups while multiple basing elements counterbalance the dramatically extended vertical lines. Roses and button spray mums are pavéd through the center while pillows of 'Green Trick' *Dianthus* and reindeer moss provide added visual weight. The triadic color harmony of orange, green and violet is expressed in zones, with orange *Alstroemeria* on top; violet asters, *Liatris* and *Veronica* in the center; and orange and green basing elements at the bottom. Pussy willow adds stature and subtle framing, creating boundaries to hold attention within.

Sheltering is prevalent in this vegetative variation representing the understory of a wooded ravine. Moss, bark and gravel create the natural foundation at the base of the saucer, with bird's-nest fern and button fern plants enhancing the depiction of the forest floor. Spray roses and miniature *Gerbera* sprout from crevices between the green elements, adding vibrant dots of color along an informal zigzag path. Stems of fantail willow and pussy willow lie across the saucer as if fallen timber while a light veil of plumosa fern uplifts the canopy.

BOTANICAL DESIGN

Botanical designs exhibit the influence of nature by focusing on a single botanical specimen in multiple stages of development (ripening bud, emerging flower, fully open bloom, declining blossom) and revealing several different plant parts (leaves, stems, buds, flowers, pods, bulbs, roots). Other secondary floral elements may be added, but they should not compete with the botanical specimen, which serves as the focal point. The featured flower should be presented as if growing, typically with radial stem placements and all blooms occurring at a similar height. Compared to the vegetative style, this design has a more narrow focus, honing in on one flower from the garden rather than the garden in entirety.

This botanical design showcases the Asiatic lily in multiple stages of development, from bud to fully open flower. All stems emerge from the center as if coming from the same plant. Branches frame the flowers while adding texture and extending the line. The floral foam base is covered with sheet moss, with accents of bark, stones and chartreuse reindeer moss providing an unobtrusive natural finish.

LANDSCAPE DESIGN

The landscape design style depicts the largest scope of a natural landscape, with flowers, foliages, branches, bark, rocks, moss and other natural elements used to depict a realistic scene, including trees, shrubs, garden plants, pathways, ponds and riverbeds. Man-made elements are sometimes included, such as benches, arbors or stepping stones fashioned from sticks, stones and other natural materials. Unlike the vegetative and botanical styles, which attempt to portray nature in its purest sense, here, the noticeable influence of the florist as "landscape designer" is acceptable.

Branched stems of *Nandina* form a tree-like canopy over this landscape design, with framing lines of fantail willow contributing height and drama to the upper story. Midlevel *Leucadendron* and *Grevillea* serve as small trees or large shrubs while the man-made landscape is dotted with shrub-like clusters of Oregonia, *Acacia*, and *Hypericum*, with 'Lemonade' roses and 'Green Trick' *Dianthus* filling out the base. Micro spray mums mimic annuals while a collection of bark, moss, pods and dried split peas enhance the texture and cover mechanics.

HEDGEROW DESIGN

The hedgerow design style is so named because of its similarity to a row of trees or shrubs along a roadside or separating areas of a formal garden. Sometimes compared to an English Becher's Brook, the style is characterized by terraced groupings of flowers forming a vertical wall. In this style, flowers are placed in consistent parallel rows, with the resulting composition forming a solid, boxy mass. Though typically devoid of a focal point, this design benefits from an accent such as an unexpected color or a sharply contrasting textural element. By placing the accent off-center, the asymmetry of nature is highlighted.

Zones of larkspur, *Liatris* and heather provide a three-tiered hedgerow anchored by a thick base of boxwood and seeded *Eucalyptus*. Curly willow extends the line and breaks up the monotony of the vertical lines and parallel placements. A horizontal line of gnarled OASIS™ Rustic Wire provides visual separation between layers while terraced lotus pods and a fibrous root provide unexpected accents in keeping with the garden inspiration of the composition.

WATERFALL DESIGN

The waterfall design is a nature-inspired style with strong cascading lines that mimic the flow of water over the edge of a cliff. Floral materials are designed in layers, using the veiling technique to create a see-through shelter effect over portions of the design. The bottom layers of the waterfall should flow directly downward while the uppermost layers flow from the back of the design over the top. All layers should maintain a consistent width, tapering the volume of materials toward the tip. Reflective materials including beads, decorative wire and mirror chips are sometimes used to imitate the reflection of sunlight on water while OASIS™ Rustic Wire, yarn, dried leaves and bark are suitable additions to replicate elements that have floated downstream.

The mass of a single football mum anchors the center of this waterfall design, providing visual stability as bells-of-Ireland, miniature callas, *Freesia* and Queen Anne's lace flow freely in this lightly layered composition. Hanging *Amaranthus* leaps forward from the back as do individual blades of lily grass and arching stems of plumosa fern. The flowing lines are distinctly downward and are enhanced by kinked and coiled lines of OASIS™ Rustic Wire, which repeats the chocolate color of the container and adds complexity to the design's cascading rhythm.

Chapter Four

HOLIDAY & NOVELTY DESIGNS

Holidays and special occasions provide opportunities to design flowers with familiar themes, unique shapes and sometimes a sense of humor. A birthday is more special with a slice of floral cake, and Valentine's Day is more romantic with flowers designed to form a heart. Cute containers or playful accessories can make an ordinary arrangement more spirited and memorable. Flowers with faces always evoke smiles. Here, we provide inspiration for holiday and novelty designs with both current and classic appeal.

BOXWOOD TREE

Fresh boxwood trees are a holiday staple in many flower shops. Whether plain or decorated, they are a favored winter holiday decoration that mimics the Christmas tree in miniature. OASIS® Floral Foam Cones provide the perfect foundation to achieve an even and well-proportioned shape. Fresh flowers, berries and small pine cones can be added, if desired. Here, a modern approach is demonstrated using OASIS™ Etched Wire and OASIS™ MEGA Beaded Wire.

SUGGESTED MATERIALS:

Boxwood

OASIS® Floral Foam Cone

OASIS® Floral Foam Maxlife

OASIS™ Etched Wire

OASIS™ MEGA Beaded Wire

4" and 6" Wireless Wood Picks

Fill an upright container with soaked OASIS® Floral Foam Maxlife so it fits tightly within. Trim the foam level with the top of the container. Insert a 6-inch wireless wood pick in the center of the foam, then add three 4-inch wireless wood picks around it.

Soak an OASIS® Floral Foam Cone in flower food solution, and place it in the center of the container so the wood picks are inserted fully and the base of the cone rests on the floral foam base.

Insert a linear stem of boxwood into the top of the floral foam cone to establish the height. Add short stems of boxwood horizontally around the base of the cone so they extend about 1 inch to 1½ inches beyond the container edge. Place the stems close together to create a dense mass of greens.

Continue adding boxwood from the base upward. As the greens reach the midsection of the cone, insertions should begin to shift from horizontal to more upward angles.

Fill the remainder of the cone with boxwood, increasing the upward angles of insertion as the greens reach the top. Stem length should remain consistent – about 1 inch to 1 ½ inches throughout the cone.

Insert the end of a coil of OASIS™ Etched Wire into the cone, near the base. Then, wind the wire around the cone, working up to the top and then back down to the base, allowing the wire to overlap randomly.

Unwind 1 to 2 yards of OASIS™ MEGA Beaded Wire, and wrap it around the cone following the same up and down process as the etched wire. Create depth by tucking some of the beads deep among the greens and keeping others on the surface. Wire a bead to the top piece of boxwood to complete the design.

EVERGREEN WREATH

A decorated door wreath provides a welcome greeting during the holiday season. Pine cones, berries and baubles are common decorative elements, along with festive ribbons and bows. Evergreen options including pine, fir, cedar and juniper can be used alone or mixed with other types of greens to create a variety of looks. Boxwood, with its small leaves, makes a nice accent to traditional needled evergreens. Here, we demonstrate the wreath-making process using soft, pliable and long-lasting fir.

SUGGESTED MATERIALS:

- Fresh Evergreen Boughs
- Permanent Botanical Foliage
- Pine Cones
- Plastic Holiday Balls
- Wire Wreath Frame
- Artificial Stemmed Berries
- Atlantic® Traditional Chenille Stems
- Waxed String

DESIGN STEPS

Tie the end of a spool of waxed string to one of the support wires that crosses from the inner to the outer wreath circle. Attach the string so it cannot slide along the rounded frame. Make bundles of evergreens, each with three to six stems about 7 to 9 inches in length. All stems in the bundles should be positioned in the same direction.

Position one evergreen bundle on the wire frame, and wrap the waxed string around the stems three or four times, pulling it taut. Keep the string attached to the spool.

Add a second bundle, placing the top of it over the stems of the first bundle and wrapping with the continuous spool of waxed string. Add a third bundle in the same manner. Adjust the bundles as needed so the greens cover the sides as well as the top of the wreath frame.

Continue adding evergreen bundles to cover the wreath. To add the last bundle, lift the first bundle and insert the stems underneath. Bind the bundle in place, then tie the string to the nearest support wire that spans the circular frame.

Prepare pine cones by twisting a brown chenille stem around each cone so it wraps deep within the scales. Twist the ends of the chenille stem together to secure the wire in place. Use the chenille stems to attach the pine cones to the wreath frame in groups of two or three.

Insert the stems of permanent botanical foliage into the network of greens among the pine-cone groupings. Use OASIS® Hot-melt Glue or OASIS® Floral Adhesive, as needed, to secure the leaves in place.

Prepare the ornaments by securing the ornament caps with glue and adding chenille stems to the wire atop the caps. Then, wire the ornaments to the wreath frame, mixing the colors and applying them singly and in pairs.

Repeat Step 6 to add the wired berry stems among the pine-cone groupings.

Create a multiloop bow using No. 40 ribbon. Secure the bow with a chenille stem, keeping the ribbon attached to the bolt. Choose a space between the pine-cone clusters to secure the bow to the wreath.

Use the ribbon, still attached to the bolt, to extend a rhythmic line around the wreath. Secure the ribbon intermittently by twisting a chenille stem around the ribbon and then attaching the chenille stem to the wreath frame.

Position the ribbon, as needed, to unify the other wreath components. Fluff the loops of the bow, and trim any evergreens that fill the center opening or extend too far beyond the outer wreath edge.

TRADITIONAL SWAG

Holiday swags come in many shapes and sizes. Some are horizontal collections of evergreens designed to be hung over the door. Variations of this style include pointed ovals and crescents or arches. Other swags are teardrop shaped, with elongated versions reminiscent of a cascade bouquet. This classic style involves simple construction of evergreen boughs gathered into a bundle and embellished as desired.

SUGGESTED MATERIALS:

Fir

Cedar

Arborvitae

Mountain Hemlock or Balsam Fir

Pine Cones

Atlantic® Traditional Chenille Stems

OASIS™ Raw Jute

Choose three branched stems of mountain hemlock or similar evergreens with naturally tapered shapes. Position a long pointed stem in the center. Arrange the other two stems, slightly shorter than the first, on each side of center.

Stack three shorter stems on top of the first trio, aligning all of the stems into a unit. The bundle should begin to develop some depth in the center. If it is flat, add two or three additional stems.

Add two or three stems of a contrasting evergreen, such as cedar or arborvitae, which have flat scale-like leaves that contrast with the needled greens. Stack the contrasting greens on top of the mountain hemlock bundle, and align the stems with the rest.

Use a green chenille stem to bind the stems tightly together. The ends of the chenille can be twisted to form a looped hanger.

Prepare pine cones by twisting a brown chenille stem around each cone so it wraps deep within the scales. Twist the ends of the chenille stem together to secure the wire in place. Use the chenille to attach a pine cone to a sturdy evergreen branch in the center of the swag.

Add a pine cone, slightly higher than the first, on each side of the center cone. Angle these cones away from the center cone, and secure tightly with chenille stems.

Create a multiloop bow using 2-inch OASIS™ Raw Jute ribbon. Secure three to five streamers into the bow using a chenille stem, then twist the chenille around the evergreen stems. Position the streamers between the pine cones.

Anchor the streamers into position by twisting a chenille stem around each piece of ribbon a few inches from the end, then twist the chenille around the branches. Position and bind the streamers so they have some natural drape and flow.

Fluff the ribbon loops, and trim the evergreen stems into a neat unit, to complete the design.

EVERGREEN GARLAND

Garlands are versatile holiday decorations. Whether draping a doorway, wrapped up a staircase, or festooned across a mantel, an evergreen garland adds holiday flair indoors or out. Strung down the center of a table, a garland makes a no-fuss centerpiece. Wrapped in a spiral, a garland turns a stately column into a festive candy cane.

Garland-making options abound. Some are thin, wispy and unembellished. Others are thick, luxurious and heavily adorned. Whether mixed or monobotanical, the choice of evergreens will greatly influence the look of the finished result, as will the length and fullness of the foliage bundles. Here, we demonstrate a dense garland of silver fir, arborvitae and mountain hemlock.

SUGGESTED MATERIALS:

Mountain Hemlock or Balsam Fir

Silver Fir

Arborvitae

20-gauge OASIS™ Spool Wire or OASIS™ Paddle Wire

22-, 23- or 24-gauge OASIS™ Spool Wire or OASIS™ Paddle Wire

DESIGN STEPS

1. Create a dozen or more bundles of evergreens, making sure to stack the greens consistently in a sequence such as hemlock-fir-arborvitae. Strive for bundles that are about the same length and fullness. Using two spools or paddles of wire, one 20 gauge and the other 22, 23 or 24 gauge, bind both wires around a single bundle of evergreens.

2. Position a second evergreen bundle so the tips cover the stems of the first. Use the lighter wire to wrap tightly around the bundle three or four times. The heavier wire will serve to create a continuous spine throughout the length of the garland. Be sure to wrap the lighter gauge wire around the heavier spine wire as well as the greens.

3. Repeat Step 2 with all but one of the remaining bundles. Strive for consistent spacing and variety in the side-to-side placement of the different types of greens.

Add the last bundle, with the stems turned in the opposite direction from the rest, making sure to hide the stems underneath the greens. Wrap the bundle three or four times with the lighter wire, then twist the two wire spools or paddles around each other to secure both the wrapping wire and the spine wire before clipping off the spools/paddles. Tuck the wire ends deep into the evergreens.

The finished garland should be pliable enough to bend or festoon, and full enough that there are no gaps when draped.

GRAVE BLANKET

Grave blankets made of evergreens are a winter season tradition in northern states. Symbolic of warm remembrance, families typically place grave blankets at the cemetery in November or December, where they remain until early spring. They can be made by stapling greens to a wood base, inserting greens into Styrofoam, or threading greens through OASIS™ Florist Netting (chicken wire). Landscape staples, available from garden or hardware stores, are an effective attachment method to secure grave blankets to the ground. These heavy-gauge two-prong stakes of galvanized steel can be inserted through the base or across the boughs to hold the blanket in place.

The styling of grave blankets varies from one source to the next. Most have dimensions somewhat smaller than the gravesite, averaging 4 to 5 feet in length and 24 to 36 inches in width. Some are designed in a rectangular shape, with a flat profile. Others are more tapered at the ends and mounded in the center. While evergreens are the primary ingredient, accessories including pine cones, dried pods, ribbon and decorative accents are often added to provide color and interest. Here, the chicken-wire method is used to create a holiday-inspired grave blanket with a tapered shape.

SUGGESTED MATERIALS:

- Silver or Noble Fir
- Balsam or Douglas Fir or Mountain Hemlock
- Cedar or Arborvitae
- Pine Cones
- No. 40 Ribbon
- OASIS™ Florist Netting

DESIGN STEPS

1.

Form a length of chicken wire into a large loop, allowing the ends to overlap several inches. Use a long stem of fir to secure the chicken wire by threading it from the underside of the loop through openings in the lower and then the upper layers. Thread the stem back through the upper layer to finish the "stitch" and hold the chicken wire in place.

2.

Repeat Step 1 with a similar piece of fir on the opposite end of the chicken wire, to establish the length of the blanket. While "stitching," the chicken wire may become somewhat flattened. Pull the two layers of chicken wire apart as needed to maintain separate layers.

3.

On both ends of the design, add a pair of slightly shorter stems of fir on each side of the "stitched" stem. Angle these stems toward the corners of the chicken wire frame. Add a short stem of fir extending horizontally from the center of the frame. Repeat on the opposite side to establish the tapered, pointed oval outline.

4.

Fill in the spaces with additional stems of fir to complete the outline. Vary the stem lengths to maintain the pointed-oval shape. Position these stems horizontally so they will rest on the ground.

5.

Place additional stems of fir into the top of the frame, radiating them from the center outward in each direction until the center is full and the chicken wire is no longer visible. The network of stems will become secure as more are added and they become interlocked with each other.

6.

Turn the grave blanket upside down, and insert short pieces of fir to cover the chicken wire and prevent scratching. In this image, the right half is complete, and the left half awaits coverage.

7.

Turn the blanket right side up, and add one or two additional types of evergreen to fill out the shape and add texture.

8.

Add pine cones using wire or chenille stems to secure them to the boughs. Place the pine cones in pairs and trios so they radiate from the center outward.

9.

Create a multiloop bow with streamers using No. 40 ribbon, and wire it into the center of the design. Thread the streamers through the evergreens to enhance the radial lines and extend the color to the edges of the design.

SUGGESTED MATERIALS:

Leucospermum
Leucadendron
Larkspur
Spray Roses
Micro Spray (Pompon) Chrysanthemums
Craspedia
Hypericum
Statice
Solidago
Salal
Italian *Ruscus*
Sword Fern
Fresh Wheat
Carrots
Onion
Radishes
Asparagus
Sweet Potatoes
OASIS™ Double Bowl
OASIS® Waterproof Tape
Atlantic® Traditional Chenille Stems
Wood Picks

CORNUCOPIA CENTERPIECE

The cornucopia, symbolic of abundance, makes a fitting container for a Thanksgiving centerpiece. The traditional horn-of-plenty is filled with fruits, vegetables, nuts and grains. When combined with fresh flowers, preserved leaves and dried pods, the fall harvest theme is further enhanced.

When choosing fruits and vegetables for a cornucopia centerpiece, choose types that offer a variety of colors and forms. Carrots and celery provide line; onions, apples or pomegranates provide mass; miniature gourds or pineapples provide form; and grapes, radishes and Brussels sprouts make good fillers. Sliced kiwis or citrus fruits can add interest to a centerpiece intended for short-term use, but as a rule, seek produce that has a stable shelf life without refrigeration.

Cornucopias are often made of wicker, vines or similar basket-like materials. The round opening and curved tip mimics a goat's horn. Some, designed specifically for flower arranging, have an extended lip that supports a tray where floral foam can be secured. In the absence of such a tray, a liner must be attached to the cornucopia to provide a design base.

Here, we demonstrate a method to achieve a festive fall centerpiece in a lipless cornucopia. For a natural look, the cornucopia is enhanced with wraps of OASIS™ Rustic Wire and tucks of sheet moss.

DESIGN STEPS

Tape OASIS® Floral Foam Maxlife into a narrow utility container. Bevel the end of the foam that will be inserted into the cornucopia. Position a chenille stem under the container and another one over it, and twist the ends together.

Insert the container into the cornucopia as far as it will go. Thread the ends of the chenille stems through the weave of the cornucopia, and twist the ends together to secure the container in place. Bend the chenille stems back into the interior of the cornucopia. Cover any visible chenille with tucks of sheet moss.

Green up the container with mixed foliages and grains. Extend a strong horizontal line about 1.5 times the length of the cornucopia, then use shorter horizontal pieces to broaden the silhouette. Use short vertical pieces of foliage to fill in the opening of the cornucopia.

Use wood picks to prepare the fruits and vegetables, inserting the pointed end into the produce. For large or heavy produce, such as apples or onions, use a pair of picks angled away from each other to stabilize the insertions. Position linear fruits or vegetables first, following the lines of the foliage base.

Place the largest fruits or vegetables near the opening of the cornucopia, leaving space between them for flower insertions.

Add line flowers to follow the foliage outline of the design. Here, larkspur is used in pairs while a trio of 'Safari Sunset' *Leucadendron* draw the color of the red onion from the center to the tip. Spears of asparagus are bundled and bound with wire to complete the linear placements.

Anchor the center of the design with two or three focal flowers such as *Leucospermum*. Vary the facings of these flowers to provide interest from multiple perspectives.

Enhance the "horn-of-plenty" appearance by adding a variety of small-bloomed and filler flowers such as spray roses, micro spray mums, statice and *Hypericum*, limiting each to one to three stems. Add a fruit or vegetable filler, such as individually picked radishes positioned in the focal area and repeated at the tip.

Connect the filler produce placements with a few radishes through the center, then add textural fillers, such as *Solidago*, to blend and unify the elements. Globular *Craspedia* provides a playful final accent.

MAKING A FRUIT BASKET

Fruit baskets are popular gifts during the winter holiday season. Whether created with classic fruit combinations or custom designed with gourmet options, they require strategic stacking and polished packaging to create a salable result.

When selecting produce, look for fruits that are plump, shiny and blemish free. Strive for a variety of colors, sizes and shapes. Consider ripeness also, opting for green bananas, firm kiwis and under-ripe pears, for example, because ethylene gas trapped inside the wrapping can speed the ripening process.

Fruit baskets can be wrapped in cellophane or shrink wrap. Cellophane requires minimal equipment and fewer steps but may not hold the fruit in place as reliably as shrink wrap. Baskets should be prepared so all of the fruits are visible, with the heaviest and bulkiest fruits at the base.

To support the fruits, the basket interior should be filled with crumpled butcher paper, newspaper or similar. A small cardboard box is also an option. Fillers used to cover the base include crinkle-cut paper, metallic shred, tissue paper and excelsior. Nuts or wrapped candies make good fillers to tuck in the gaps between fruits. A flourish of ribbon provides the final crown.

DESIGN STEPS

1. Fill the basket with crumpled butcher paper, and top with enough crinkle-cut paper to cover.

DESIGN STEPS

Arrange fruits around the edge of the basket, varying the types and colors as well as the angles or facings of each piece. Add smaller fruits to the center. This will help with the stability of later fruit additions.

Stack a second layer of fruit atop the first, positioning more special fruits on the exterior. While stacking, use looped pieces of clear packing tape, as needed, to prevent fruits from rolling off.

Use small fruits to create a third layer.

Place a small bunch of bananas across the top. The curve and the weight of the bananas will help anchor the topmost fruits.

Add nuts to fill gaps between the fruits. Then, pull a shrink-wrap bag over the top of the basket, positioning the bag seams on the sides of the basket.

Tuck the open ends of the bag under the basket, starting from the backside of the basket and then the front. The closed end of the bag should rest against the bananas. Use clear packing tape to secure the layers under the basket. This is most easily accomplished by two people, one lifting the basket and the other taping it.

Fold the corners of the shrink wrap to the back, and secure with small pieces of clear packing tape. The tape will be less obvious if it is positioned in the area of the basket rather than the fruit.

Hold a heat gun 5 to 6 inches away from the basket, and heat the shrink wrap until it is tight against the basket. Keep the heat gun moving at all times. Briefly move in closer, if needed, to shrink the wrap until there are minimal wrinkles. Too much heat will rapidly result in large holes.

Once the film around the basket is tight, heat the wrap around the fruit using the same constant motion and quick bursts of heat closer to the wrap.

As the wrap shrinks, the fruit and nuts will become secure. Be careful not to heat it so much that the fruit is pulled out of the desired positions.

Continue heating until most wrinkles are eliminated. If a wrinkled area resists shrinking, move to another area, and return to it after a few seconds of cooling.

The finished shrink wrap will be about 80% to 90% smooth. Wrinkles are most likely to occur on the sides where the shrink wrap was folded back and taped over itself.

Create a multiloop bow with No. 9 ribbon. Design the bow with at least 20 loops, all of the same size, and secure it with 24-gauge wire. Spiral the wire into a flat circular formation, and use clear packing tape to secure the spiral under the loops.

FRUIT BASKET VARIATION USING CELLOPHANE

Cellophane is available in colors and prints that create a multitude of options for fruit basket themes. Still, clear cellophane is used most often so the fruit is easily visible. Unlike shrink wrap, cellophane will not shrink and tighten around a fruit basket when heated. Thus, the wrapping method varies, resulting in a gift basket look with a pouf of cellophane on top. Here, a different combination of fruit is used, capping the basket with delicate grapes and filling in with chocolates.

Cut a piece of cellophane to a length equal to the diameter of the basket, plus 2 x the expected height of the basket, plus 2 x 8 to 10 inches for the pouf on top). Place the cut cellophane across a table, and position the basket in the center. Prepare the basket with butcher paper and excelsior, then create the fruit base, using the largest fruits in this layer.

Stack smaller fruits to create the second and third layers. Use loops of clear packing tape, if needed, to hold fruits in place. Top with a bunch of grapes, and add wrapped chocolates in the gaps.

Pull the ends of the cellophane above the basket so the edges meet.

Cinch the cellophane together just above the fruit, and secure with a chenille stem.

Neatly fold the resulting corners from the sides toward the back of the basket, doubling the folds and securing with clear packing tape as low as possible.

Trim the ends of the chenille stem, and tie a piece of No. 9 ribbon into a shoestring bow to cover it. Trim the pouf to desired proportions, and separate the layers of cellophane to create an even, fluffy top.

This sweet heart-shaped design combines everyday flowers with decorative wire for a Valentine expression suitable for all ages. White button spray mums with close spacing provide a puffy central heart outlined with carnations and waxflower, with a Larkspur accent. OASIS™ Etched Wire forms the heart outline, and a twisted mass of OASIS™ Beaded Wire accentuates the stem and point. Placing the heart on an angle showcases it for maximum visibility.

VALENTINE'S DAY NOVELTIES

Valentine's Day provides opportunities to create sweet, charming and romantic flower arrangements. While many choose the classic vase of roses to express their love and affection, others preferring something cute or original will appreciate a novelty design.

This Valentine heart creates a frame for the delicate floral composition within. Pink OASIS™ Midollino Sticks are wrapped with purple OASIS™ Aluminum Wire and ruby OASIS™ Etched Wire to form two pieces that create the illusion of a complete heart. The upper lobed portion of the two-part heart is inserted into both sides of the container while the lower "V"-shaped portion is inserted into the front and bent downward against the surface of the container. A pair of bicolor *Anthurium* form a romantic couple flanked by miniature *Gerbera* in a field of sweet peas, *Boronia*, waxflower and statice. Craft-foam hearts, glued back to back with florist wire in between, create simple accents that reinforce the theme.

CLASSIC ICE-CREAM SODA

Among the many food-related floral novelties, the ice-cream soda is a classic that has broad appeal. When designed in pink to mimic a strawberry soda, it makes a charming Valentine's Day offering. At other times of year, the colors can be shifted to imitate many flavors. Follow these simple instructions to create a quick ice-cream soda.

Fill a soda glass about half full with flower food solution. Add one or two drops of red food coloring, and stir.

Fill the glass with white shredded Styrofoam. Use a straw to push the foam into the water and to the bottom of the glass.

Fill the top of the glass with short stems of baby's breath, arranging it primarily around the edges. Make sure the stems are hidden within the Styrofoam so no stems are visible.

Add four carnations so they rest on top of the baby's breath. The carnations and baby's breath should both extend over the edges of the soda glass.

Use a florist knife to make a slit near the base of two plastic drinking straws. The slits assure that the straws will not function, preventing accidental consumption of the flower food solution

Add a single white carnation in the middle of the pink ones. Accent the carnation with a red sweetheart rose, single spray rose or a plastic cherry. Insert the two straws among the carnations, and display on a paper doily.

FLORAL DESSERT VARIATIONS

With a little ingenuity, flowers can be fashioned into a broad menu of desserts. Using similar techniques to the ice-cream soda, quick and easy designs, with broad consumer appeal, are possible. Let these variations be a springboard to new and original ideas suitable for many cheerful occasions.

Sherbet-colored carnations fill this soda glass, demonstrating the ease of varying flower colors to achieve different effects. Here, baby's breath is omitted, and a cherry replaces the rose, to create a colorful companion to the strawberry soda.

Ice-cream cartons burst with tasty floral treats in this design concept by Beth Zsoldos. On the left, chartreuse button spray mums cover a three-inch floral foam sphere and are accented by green *Hypericum* berries and a dollop of baby's breath posing as whipped cream. On the right, white button spray mums are similarly mounded and sprinkled with colorful candies and miniature peanut butter cups. Artificial berries act as cherries. A lined and foam-filled ice-cream cone filled with spray (miniature) carnations rests below.

A wedge of Oasis foam provides the perfect foundation for this tasty slice of floral cake. White button mums are lined up to create cake layers while roses, pepper berries, waxflower and babies' breath ice the top and sides. Red aluminum wire twisted into a wide ribbon provides the "filling" between the layers.

Spray roses and spray (miniature) carnations provide the icing on this floral cupcake. By collaring the cupcake container with roses and mounding spray carnations over the top, a cupcake shape is achieved. A rose in the center serves as a fitting candleholder.

FLORAL PETS AND CRITTERS

Whether pets or critters, flowers formed into any number of animals or insects create conversation and smiles. Place one of these designs in the display cooler or on the flower shop website, and they're bound to generate questions, comments and positive buzz. When creating flowers with faces, pay careful attention to the spacing between the eyes. Too close together or too far apart will create a look that is dazed or confused.

PETITE PUP

Across the floral industry, there are many iterations of the floral pup. Often appearing much like a poodle, this cute design can be created with a full body or just a head. Here, it is portrayed as if lying in a flower garden.

SUGGESTED MATERIALS:

- Football Chrysanthemums
- Daisy Spray (Pompon) Chrysanthemums
- Mini Spray (Pompon) Chrysanthemums
- Spray (Miniature) Carnations
- *Aster* 'Monte Cassino'
- Leatherleaf Fern
- Huckleberry
- No. 2-3 Ribbon
- 26-gauge OASIS™ Florist Wire
- OASIS® Floral Adhesive
- Light Pink and Black Atlantic® Traditional Chenille Stems
- Plastic Craft Eyes

Place soaked floral foam in a medium-sized basket, and green up with leatherleaf and huckleberry. Add a single football mum just below the handle. Add a second football mum so it rests just beneath the first so that the top mum overlaps with it.

From the front view, the two mums should form the beginning of a face, with the lower mum forming the jowls. Ideally, choose a mum with an upright facing for the top bloom and one with an angled facing for the lower one.

Add a sideward-facing football mum on each side of the facial flowers. Position them like muffs to form the ears. Be sure to place them closely so there are no gaps.

Place two football mums side by side centered beneath the head. Allow a small gap between these flowers and the ones above.

Make two matching corsage bows. Apply OASIS® Floral Adhesive to the base of one bow, and slide the wire between the topmost mum and an "ear" flower on the side. Repeat on the opposite side. Glue two plastic craft eyes to the lower forward-facing mum, in the area where the top flower overlaps it.

Add a football mum to form the back of the head. Then, use three mums below it to form the haunches, centering one of the mums and positioning the others on each side. Add a spray carnation bloom from below the center mum, with enough length to form a tail.

Shape a piece of black chenille stem into a solid triangle to form a nose, then glue the triangle upside down below the eyes using floral adhesive. Bend a pink chenille stem to form a "U" shape, then bend the chenille further to fill in the "U." Arch the pink "U" to create a tongue, and glue it among the petals slightly beneath the nose.

Arrange the spray mums, spray carnations and *Aster* 'Monte Cassino' scattered throughout the base to unify the pup with the basket.

This trio of baby novelties demonstrates potential color palettes. When the gender of the baby is not known, pink and blue can be paired together or enhanced, as shown in the center design, with neutral whites and cheerful yellows.

BABY NOVELTIES

C.

New-baby arrangements are the quintessential novelty designs. Often arranged in novelty containers, the vessels in which they are designed often provide instant floral design themes. There is rarely confusion about the occasion for an arrangement designed in a baby bottle or a diaper-wrapped vase. Container shapes, motifs and colors send clear messages, and the flowers designed within reinforce them.

Baby arrangements should generally be soft colored and delicately textured. Proportions are often petite, which suits many of the novelty containers that are small or have small openings. The limited table space in hospital rooms also suits these moderate proportions.

The decision to design baby novelties in one-sided or all-around styles may be dependent on the container shape. Many novelty containers are decorated with a clearly defined front and back. For those containers, one-sided styles make sense. When designing in novelty containers, keep in mind that often, once the flowers perish, the container will become a nursery decoration or keepsake. Mechanics should not mar the container interior or exterior.

A. A baby block provides a comparable container to the common glass floral cube. This one-sided isosceles triangle showcases a broad flower mix, using only two to three of most flower types to keep the proportions in check. When the designer lacks knowledge of the baby's gender, pink and blue can be paired together or enhanced as shown, with neutral whites and cheerful yellows.

B. This diminutive design features blush tulips in a sea of baby pink spray carnations and warm pink waxflower, fluffy baby's breath and delicate plumosa fern are the perfect filler elements to provide a feminine finish.

C. This upright baby booty variation uses blue *Delphinium* to provide the central vertical line while white cushion spray mums anchor the base. Spiral *Eucalyptus* and deep blue statice fill out the shape and provide pleasing color and textural contrasts.

SEASONAL AND ALL-OCCASION NOVELTIES

PUMPKIN

Though often associated with holidays and life events, novelties can be enjoyed year-round. Whether for a special occasion or just because, novelties bring smiles and create conversation. Here, a collection of spirited seasonal and all-occasion novelties provides a springboard of creative design ideas.

An OASIS™ Wood Cube sets the stage for this vine-ripened autumn novelty. Using a 6-inch OASIS® Floral Foam Sphere secured with hyacinth stakes into the foam-filled container, the pumpkin form is achieved with one bunch (25) of fluffy orange carnations. Multiple lengths of OASIS™ Rustic Wire are twisted to form a stem while a gnarled handful of OASIS™ Bind Wire creates a straw-like understory. Seeded *Eucalyptus* lends a natural foliage accent, contributing both color and textural contrast.

NOVELTY CONTAINERS AND ACCESSORIES

Novelty arrangements are often referred to as such when designed in novelty containers or enhanced with novel accessories. The skillful designer must balance the cute themes or playful qualities of these design components with the tasteful use of materials and the principles and elements of floral design. Flowers should remain the focus, with the novel contributions of the container or accessories as secondary components. Unity is the key. Without it, a design in a novelty container or incorporating novel accessories can appear haphazard or confused.

This trio of playful novelty designs demonstrates good unity within each arrangement and also between the three unique yet coordinated, pieces.

A. The smiling mug is a floristry staple that never seems to go out of style. Cheerful yellow flowers designed with a sense of exuberance are a fitting choice. Here, clipped segments of bells-of-Ireland provide a ruffled container edge from which the *Solidago* and *Alstroemeria* emerge with a strong sense of radial rhythm. *Craspedia* springs forth to add extra bounce to this happy handful.

B. Bees buzz through this vertical composition of bells-of-Ireland, carnations and 'Green Trick' *Dianthus*. Allowing them to face in all directions, including backward, the bees seem less staged and more at home among the flowers. *Solidago* filler repeats the color of their yellow bodies, and a pair of coordinating pinwheels implies a breezy motion. Plumosa fern adds softness, repeating the fuzzy texture of the chenille-stem torsos.

C. A novelty container with a face should always be treated as an important part of a design. Here, the lonely lion's expression is prominent, with matching *Gerbera* repeating the colors and patterns of his markings. The low and rounded design sits comfortably on the lion's back while OASIS™ Bind Wire is cleverly formed into a tail for a whimsical finish.

Floral design by Kelly Shore of Petals by the Shore
Photo by Kathleen Dillinger for Wildflower Media, Inc.

Chapter Five

FLOWERS TO WEAR

Fresh flowers, designed as corsages, boutonnières, and hair accessories are some of the smallest arrangements made by florists. These special-occasion flowers require great care in preparing and assembling the components into thoughtfully tailored fashion accessories. It is hard to imagine that the full complement of floral design principles could be employed in such diminutive compositions, yet without appropriate proportion, good balance and notable focal emphasis, to name a few, flowers to wear may disappoint.

The mechanics for designing flowers to wear have evolved as new products have been introduced into the floral industry. Modern floral adhesives can simplify much of the design process. Nevertheless, wiring and taping are still essential skills that a floral designer must master to be versatile and adaptable to clients' needs. In this chapter, a variety of mechanical methods are demonstrated, with the intention of providing information that designers can use to adapt techniques to each situation based on the specific flower types and design styles requested.

WIRING & TAPING FLOWERS

When designing flowers to wear, wire serves multiple purposes. It creates flexibility so that each flower or leaf can be maneuvered into the desired position. When properly wired, a flower can be bent to nearly any angle. This is important in the transition of flower facings from the top through the center to the base of a design. Wire also aids in the ability to position foliage so that it provides a sufficient background and hides the mechanics. Wire serves as a replacement for the natural flower or foliage stems, which are often somewhat rigid. The removal of the natural stems, typically leaving no more than one inch beneath the flower, reduces bulk as designs are assembled, creating a finished product that is lighter in weight and more sleek in appearance.

Standard florist wire is typically 18 inches in length. For most flowers to wear, less length is required, so cutting wire in half will maximize use. The weight of florist wire is identified by numbered gauges, with 16-gauge wire being the heaviest and 30-gauge wire the lightest. For most corsage and boutonnière designs, gauges 22, 23, 24, 26 and 28 are most useful. Generally, a designer should use the lightest-weight wire that will support the flower or foliage. This will ensure a lightweight finished product.

Each flower or foliage should be wired using the appropriate method. The chart that follows provides the wire gauge and wiring method most suited to common corsage flowers. Step-by-step instructions illustrate common and specialized wiring methods.

WIRING CHART

This wiring chart provides a convenient list of selected flowers and foliages suitable for flowers to wear. The recommended wire gauges and wiring techniques may be adjusted to suit each design situation.

FOLIAGE

FOLIAGE	GAUGE	TECHNIQUE
Bear Grass	26	Wraparound
Boxwood	24	Wraparound
Camellia	24	Stitch
Eucalyptus Seeded (seed cluster)	26	Wraparound
Eucalyptus Seeded (leaf)	26	Stitch
Eucalyptus Silver Dollar	26	Stitch
Eucalyptus Spiral (tip)	26	Wraparound
Foxtail Fern (tip)	26	Wraparound
Geranium	26	Stitch
Ivy	26	Stitch
Leatherleaf Fern	26	Hairpin

FOLIAGE	GAUGE	TECHNIQUE
Ming Fern (cluster)	26	Wraparound
Myrtle (tip)	24	Wraparound
Oregonia	26	Wraparound
Pittosporum (cluster)	26	Hairpin
Pittosporum (leaf)	24	Stitch
Plumosa Fern	28	Wraparound
Ruscus Israeli	26	Stitch
Ruscus Italian (cluster)	26	Wraparound
Ruscus Italian (leaf)	28	Stitch
Salal	26	Stitch
Sprengeri Fern (cluster)	26	Wraparound

FLOWERS

FLOWER	GAUGE	TECHNIQUE
Acacia (cluster)	26	Wraparound
Agapanthus (single bloom)	28	Pierce
Ageratum	26	Wraparound
Allium (Drumstick)	24	Insertion

FLOWER	GAUGE	TECHNIQUE
Alstroemeria (single bloom)	28	Pierce
Amaranthus	24	Wraparound
Aster	24	Insertion
Aster 'Monte Cassino' (cluster)	26	Wraparound

FLOWER	GAUGE	TECHNIQUE
Astilbe	26	Wraparound
Baby's Breath (cluster)	28	Wraparound
Boronia (cluster)	26	Wraparound
Bouvardia	26	Hairpin
Bupleurum	26	Wraparound
Calla (Miniature)	24	Pierce
Calycina (Thryptomene)	26	Wraparound
Carnation (Spray/Miniature)	24	Pierce
Carnation (Standard)	22	Pierce
Celosia	24	Wraparound
Chrysanthemum (Button)	24	Insertion
Chrysanthemum (Cushion)	24	Insertion
Chrysanthemum (Daisy)	22	Hook
Cornflower	24	Insertion
Craspedia	24	Insertion
Dahlia	22	Insertion
Delphinium (single bloom)	26	Hairpin
Diosma	24	Wraparound
Freesia	24	Wraparound
Gardenia	24	Cross Pierce*
Genista (cluster)	26	Wraparound
Gerbera (miniature)	22	Insertion
Gladiolus (single bloom)	26	Cross Pierce
Gloriosa	24	Insertion
Godetia/Clarkia (single bloom)	26	Pierce
Heather	26	Wraparound
Hyacinth (single bloom)	28	Pierce
Hydrangea (single bloom)	26	Wraparound
Hypericum	24	Hairpin
Kangaroo Paw	26	Wraparound
Lady's Mantle (cluster)	26	Wraparound
Lavender	28	Wraparound
Larkspur (single bloom)	26	Hairpin
Leptospermum	26	Wraparound
Lilac (flower segment)	24	Wraparound
Lily	24	Pierce
Lily-of-the-Valley	28	Wraparound

FLOWER	GAUGE	TECHNIQUE
Limonium	28	Wraparound
Lisianthus/Eustoma	24	Pierce
Monkshood (single bloom)	26	Insertion
Montbretia	24	Wraparound
Narcissus	24	Insertion
Nerine (single bloom)	26	Pierce
Nigella (flower)	26	Hairpin
Nigella (pod)	26	Insertion
Orchid *Cattleya*	24	Cross Pierce*
Orchid *Cymbidium*	24	Cross Pierce*
Orchid *Dendrobium*	26	Hairpin or Pierce*
Orchid 'Japhet'	24	Cross Pierce*
Orchid *Mokara*	26	Hairpin
Orchid *Phalaenopsis*	26	Hairpin*
Orchid *Vanda*	26	Hairpin*
Peony	22	Insertion
Pepperberry (cluster)	24	Wraparound
Queen Anne's Lace	26	Hairpin
Ranunculus	24	Insertion
Rice Flower	26	Wraparound
Rose (Standard)	22	Pierce
Rose (Spray)	24	Pierce
Rose (Sweetheart)	24	Pierce
Safflower	24	Insertion
Saponaria (cluster)	28	Wraparound
Scabiosa	26	Pierce
Solidago (cluster)	26	Wraparound
Solidaster (cluster)	26	Wraparound
Star-of-Bethlehem (single bloom)	26	Pierce
Statice	26	Wraparound
Stephanotis	26	Hairpin*
Stock (single bloom)	26	Hairpin
Sweet Pea	26	Wraparound
Tuberose (single bloom)	26	Pierce
Tulip	24	Pierce
Veronica	26	Wraparound
Waxflower	26	Wraparound

*See "Wiring Techniques for Special Flowers," Pages 173-175

PIERCE WIRING

Pierce wiring is used for roses, carnations and other flowers that have large calyces or thick stems into which the wire can be inserted.

Hold a 22-gauge wire near one end, and insert it into the thickest portion of the rose calyx, just beneath the flower head.

Push the wire through the stem and out the opposite side.

Bend both ends of the wire downward, along the sides of the stem. The flower is now ready to be taped.

HOOK WIRING

The hook wiring method is used for flowers with a daisy-like center of short disc petals.

Push a 22-gauge wire through the trimmed flower stem and out the top of the flower.

Bend the top of the wire to form a shepherd's crook, with the hooked end of the wire about 3/4 inch long.

Pull the wire down until the hook pulls into the center of the flower and is hidden among the short petal-like disc flowers. The end of the wire hook should protrude from the base of the flower. When taping, it is important to catch this wire end tightly with the wrap to prevent the hook from sliding up and becoming visible in the flower center.

INSERTION WIRING

Insertion wiring is used for flowers such as button spray mums that have stems too thin to pierce and a tufted center that would be damaged by a hook.

Align a 24-gauge wire parallel to the flower stem.

Insert the wire into the base of the flower until it holds firm. The wire should not emerge from the top of the flower. When taping, wrap securely around the stem and the wire.

Alternative method: Insert the wire inside the flower stem until it reaches the flower head and is firmly in place. Then tape.

WRAPAROUND WIRING

The wraparound wiring method is used to secure multiple stems of filler flowers or foliages, such as baby's breath or ming fern, into small clusters.

Align the center of the wire with the stems of the clustered flowers, and hold between thumb and fingers.

Wrap the top half of the wire two or three times around the stems to secure the flowers into a bundle.

Complete the wire wrap by bending the ends parallel to the stems.

STITCH WIRING

Stitch wiring is used for broad-leaf foliage such as ivy and salal. A small stitch positioned just below the center of the leaf is recommended for maximum flexibility without the wire becoming visible in the finished design.

Working from the back side of the leaf, insert a 24-gauge wire horizontally through the leaf near the midrib and back through the leaf on the opposite side of the midrib, to create a small stitch.

Hold the stitch in place against the leaf with one hand while bending the wires parallel to the stem with the other hand.

Continue to hold the stitch in place while wrapping one of the wire ends around the leaf stem and the other wire end.

HAIRPIN WIRING

The hairpin wiring method is used for delicate flowers and foliage that are easily damaged when using other wiring methods.

Bend a lightweight wire in half to create the shape of a hairpin.

For blooms such as *Delphinium*, insert the ends of the hairpin wire through the center of the blossom, and pull the wire down until the bend rests behind the throat.

For leatherleaf or similar greens, straddle the bent wire across the midrib.

Hold the bent portion of the wire against the leaf with one hand while wrapping one end of the wire around the stem and the other end of the wire. Finish by aligning both ends of the wire parallel to the stem.

WIRING TECHNIQUES FOR SPECIAL FLOWERS

Most flowers and foliage can be wired using standard methods, but a few require special techniques or mechanics as described here.

STEPHANOTIS

Stephanotis *are most often sold in boxes of 25 blossoms. Flower stems are typically very short and are easily detached. Stemsons® Stay Fresh® Stephanotis Stems provide an easy way to extend stem length and add flexibility.*

1. Pull the stem and green sepals away from the flower base.

2. Use the wire end of a commercial *Stephanotis* stem to push the pistil out of the flower's center.

3. Dip the white end of the *Stephanotis* stem in water for 10 seconds, then push this end through the base of the flower.

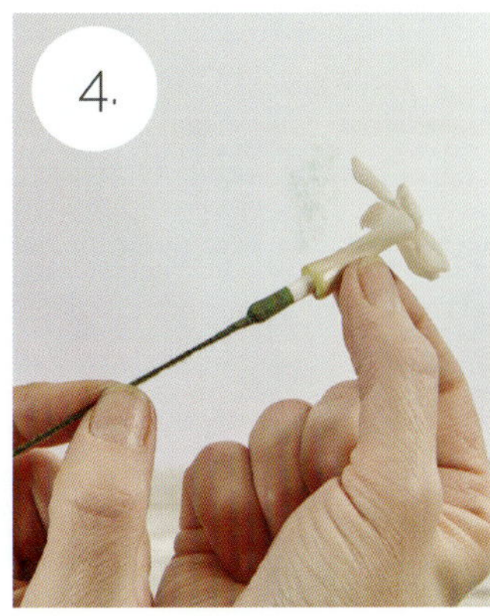
4. Use a twisting motion to ease insertion.

5. Push the stem into the flower until the taped portion reaches the flower base.

6. If desired, insert a decorative corsage pin to provide an embellishment in the center of the flower.

7. Use floral tape to secure the end of the pin to the *Stephanotis* stem (or trim the pin end with wire cutters prior to insertion so the tip does not protrude).

Alternative method: Thread a hairpin wire with a small ball of moistened cotton in the bend through the throat of the flower, and tape the wires to the intact flower stem with floral tape.

DENDROBIUM ORCHID

The hairpin wiring method can be used for **Dendrobium** ***orchids, but it may result in a visible wire in the throat of the flower. The following variation of the pierce wiring method eliminates this concern.***

Pierce a 26- or 28-gauge wire through the thick "chin" behind the lip of the orchid.

Carefully bend both wire ends so they are parallel to the flower stem.

Gently wrap one end of the wire around the flower stem and the other end of the wire.

MOKARA AND *VANDA* ORCHIDS

The wiring method for **Mokara** ***and*** **Vanda** ***orchids is a simple variation of the hairpin method. Usually, a lightweight wire, such as 26 gauge, is sufficient, but with this method a heavier wire can also be used if extra support is desired.***

Bend a wire into a hairpin shape, and position the bend at the point where the stem meets the flower.

Do not wrap the wire ends around the flower stem.

Use floral tape to secure the wire to the flower stem.

CYMBIDIUM, *CATTLEYA* AND 'JAPHET' ORCHIDS

Cymbidium, Cattleya *and 'Japhet' (*Cattleya *'Henrietta Japhet') orchids have thick stems that can be wired using the pierce method. To support the weight of the flower, often two wires are pierced in a crisscross manner.*

1. Pierce wire the orchid stem with a 22-gauge wire, then repeat with a second wire that crisscrosses the first. Bend all four wire ends parallel to the stem. Add a small moistened ball of cotton to the base of the stem, between the four wires.

2. Tape the wired stem, capturing the cotton ball within the wrap.

3. To open up the flower face and maximize the impact of *Cymbidium* orchids, gently reflex the center petal backward by pressing the curve forward from the back.

PHALAENOPSIS ORCHID

Phalaenopsis *orchids are fragile and easily bruised. The hairpin method of wiring is sometimes used, but it can involve more handling than is advisable for the delicate petals. Here is a custom method that supports the wilt-prone petals from behind.*

1. Cover an 18-inch 20-gauge wire with floral tape. Shape the wire into a mermaid's tail, with a width slightly narrower than the orchid.

2. Tape the ends of the wire together beneath the tail. Then, position the flower stem in alignment with the bound section of the wire so the tail sits behind the petals.

3. Carefully tape the flower stem to the wire. Bend the tail as needed to support the petals.

TAPING FLOWERS AND FOLIAGE

Wired flowers must be taped to stabilize and conceal the wiring. Floral tape, also known as stem wrap (Floratape® Stem Wrap is a popular brand), is available in half-inch and 1-inch widths. The half-inch width is most useful for corsages and boutonnières. Though an array of colors are available, including white, pink, red, yellow, brown, black and more, green or light green are used most often because they mimic natural stem colors and blend into the background.

Floral tape must be stretched as it is wrapped around wired stems. Stretching reveals a waxy surface quality that causes the tape to stick to itself as overlapping layers are applied. When taping, the more the tape is stretched and the less it overlaps itself as it is wrapped, the thinner, lighter and more professional the finished result will be.

Begin at the top of the wired stem, with the tape pulled taut on a downward angle.

Rotate the flower while stretching the tape, covering the wire at the top of the stem.

Stretch the tape, and pull it on a sharper angle as the flower is rotated so the tape is wrapped down the entire wire.

Tear the tape from the end of the wire. To thin and tighten the tape, hold the stem at the top and spin it with one hand while sliding the fingers of the other hand down the stem.

MAKING A BOW

Most corsages are designed with a bow. Sometimes, the difference between a boutonnière and a small corsage is simply the addition of this traditional ribbon accent. Among there are many ribbon types and sizes, No. 3-width ribbon, also referred to as corsage ribbon, is the popular choice. Thinner ribbon and even decorative wire can also be used for corsage work. A combination bow, with ribbons of two or more sizes and colors, is a showy variation. The chart below provides common ribbon sizes and their floral industry descriptors.

RIBBON NAME OR SIZE	WIDTH IN INCHES	COMMON USES
Spaghetti ribbon	1/8 inch	Corsages, hair flowers, bouquets
No. 1	1/4 inch	Corsages, hair flowers, bouquets
No. 1.5	3/8 inch	Corsages, hair flowers, bouquets
No. 2	1/2 inch	Corsages, hair flowers, bouquets
No. 3 (corsage ribbon)	5/8 inch	Corsages, hair flowers, bouquets, bud vases
No. 5	7/8 inch	Bouquets, bud vases
No. 9	1 1/2 inches	Bouquets, vase arrangements, plants
No. 16	2 1/4 inches	Vase arrangements, plants, wreaths, garlands
No. 40	3 inches	Plants, wreaths, garlands, sympathy arrangements
No. 100	4 inches	Wreaths, garlands, sympathy arrangements

CLASSIC CORSAGE BOW

The classic corsage bow has a small center loop with five or six loops on each side and two or more streamers. A typical bow measures 2-1/2 to 3-1/2 inches wide. Florist wire is used to secure the finished bow and provides a mechanism for attachment to the corsage.

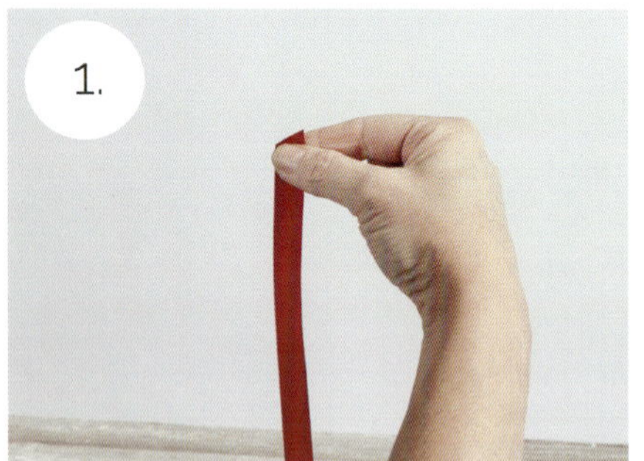

Hold the end of a length of corsage ribbon between the thumb and index finger, with the ribbon flowing downward and the shiny side of the ribbon facing away.

Loop the ribbon over the thumb, and pinch it to form the small loop that becomes the bow's center.

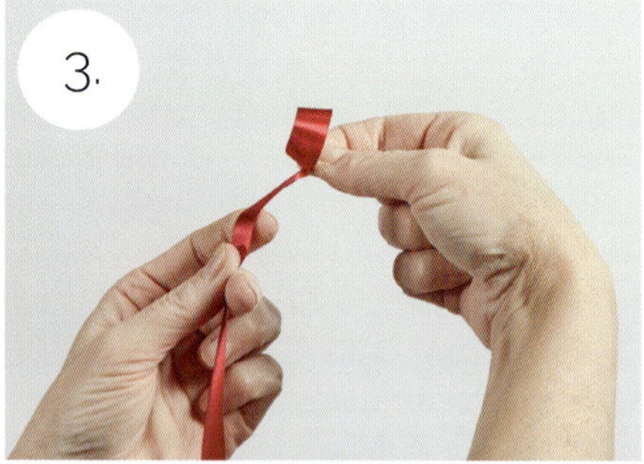

Twist the tail of the ribbon to bring the shiny side of the ribbon forward. Pinch the twisted part of the ribbon between the thumb and index finger to prevent it from untwisting.

Make a small loop (about 1 inch long) by flipping the ribbon tail back and upward. Gather the shiny side, and pinch the ribbon between the thumb and index finger.

Twist the ribbon again, and pinch the twist between the thumb and index finger to hold it in place. Flip the ribbon back and downward to make another small loop the same size as the last.

Make another pair of loops using the same process, adjusting the loop size so the second pair is about 1/4 inch wider than the first pair. With proper twisting all loops will be shiny.

With the addition of each loop, it is essential to lift the index finger slightly and then pinch again to catch the twisted portion of the ribbon in such a way that it cannot untwist as the process continues.

Make a third pair of loops about 1/4 inch larger than the last, following the same process.

As loops are added, allow them to spread apart from each other so a rounded shape begins to develop.

Add two or three more pairs of loops, keeping all loops about the same size as the third pair (1 1/2 inch).

Pinch the center of a short piece of ribbon, and add it to the pinched collection of ribbon loops to form a pair of streamers.

Insert a 24-gauge wire through the center loop, sliding it under the thumb.

Pull both ends of the wire toward the back of the bow.

Twist the wire tightly against the back of the gathered ribbon.

With thumb and index finger back in the original positions, adjust the loops as needed to form a round shape and fluffy form.

The finished bow should appear balanced from one side to the other, with the shiny side of the ribbon facing forward on all loops.

DECORATIVE WIRE BOW

Decorative spool wire can be used to design appealing bow alternatives for use in corsages and hair flowers. Available in many colors, OASIS™ Bullion Wire is a crimped type of 28-gauge wire while OASIS™ Metallic Wire is smooth 24-gauge wire. The design process is the same for making quick and easy bows with either of these wires.

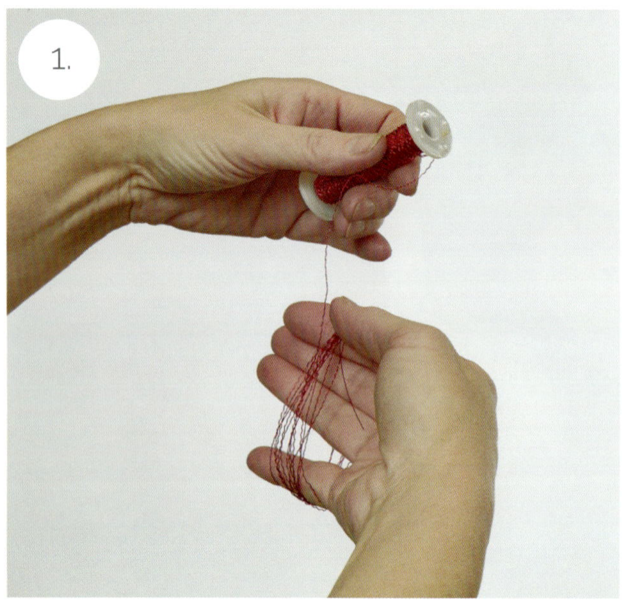

Loosely wrap Bullion Wire or Metallic Wire around one hand about 20-25 times.

Slide the wire off the hand, maintaining the looped shape.

Clip the wire to detach the spool, then pinch the loop together in the center.

Use a free end of the wire to wrap around the pinched center. Wrap several times, keeping the wire in the same central location with each wrap.

Push the two halves of the wire loops toward each other into a "V" shape.

Separate the individual wires, and spread them apart in a rounded fashion.

Twist the wire ends together to create a stem that can be used for attachment to the corsage.

CLASSIC SHOULDER CORSAGE

Corsages that are intended to be pinned to the shoulder may be designed in a variety of shapes and sizes. The classic corsage shape is tapered from tip to base, with smaller flowers near the top and larger flowers in a low central focal area. The finished design shape is similar to a small isosceles triangle.

Traditionally, pin-on corsages are designed entirely with wired and taped mechanics. In the design that follows, a hybrid approach is used, including wired elements that establish the foundation and glued elements that provide the finishing touches.

SUGGESTED MATERIALS:

Spray Roses

Dendrobium Orchids

English Ivy

Micro Spray (Pompon) Chrysanthemums

Hypericum

Waxflower

No. 2 Sheer Ribbon

Florist Wire

Floratape® Stem Wrap

OASIS® Floral Adhesive

DESIGN STEPS

Wire and tape four spray rose blooms, three *Dendrobium* orchids and eight to ten small to medium ivy leaves. Position a small ivy leaf behind the smallest spray rose, and tape it in place so the leaf tip is visible above the flower; this becomes the corsage's central spine. Position a partially open *Dendrobium* orchid to the right of the rose and a half-step lower.

Tape the orchid to the central spine starting about 1/2 inch below the base of the bloom. The 1/2 inch of stem, when left untaped, provides freedom for the orchid position to be adjusted as desired.

Position a slightly more open spray rose to the left of the first rose and a half step below the orchid. Tape the flower in the same manner as the orchid, starting about 1/2-inch below the bloom. Add an ivy leaf behind the rose so the tip is visible above the flower.

Repeat step 3 with another rose and ivy leaf on the right side of the corsage. When placing this rose, bend the top 1/2-inch of the wire slightly so the rose faces more forward than upward.

Continue the stairstepped pattern with two *Dendrobium* orchids and two ivy leaves. The lower of the two orchids should be rotated so it faces the upper orchid. Use the wire stem to arch this flower forward, achieving dominance in the focal area.

Create a corsage bow with No. 2 ribbon, and add it to the lower-left side of the corsage. The wire stem of the bow should be arched similarly to the last orchid so the binding point is hidden under the orchid and bow.

Bend an open rose to a 90-degree angle, and tuck it under the orchid and bow so it faces forward. Tape the rose at the same binding point as the bow.

This side perspective illustrates the desired development of increasing depth, achieved by shifting the flower facings from upward to outward, from the tip to the base.

Bend an ivy leaf forward and slightly to the left. Position the leaf behind the bow, and tape it to the spine.

Repeat step 9 with an ivy leaf on the right.

Add one or more ivy leaves to the back of the corsage to cover the visible taped wires.

Trim the individual stems of three micro spray mum blooms to about 1/2 to 3/4 inch in length. Apply a small amount of OASIS® Floral Adhesive to each stem, and position the blooms among the open spaces between flowers.

Repeat step 12 using individual *Hypericum* berries placed singly or in pairs.

Add small clusters of waxflower using the same glue technique. Avoid covering the roses and orchids as you place the fillers.

Spread apart the individual taped wires, and trim them with a consistent angled cut.

Adjust flower placements as needed to ensure the finished corsage will conform to the natural curve of the shoulder.

SIMPLE CORSAGES

For many occasions, the multiflower corsage is more extravagant, larger in size or more expensive than clients desire. In these situations, a single special flower can be dressed up with fillers, ribbons or other decorative accents to create a tasteful floral fashion accessory.

This trio of simple corsages showcases the design possibilities using a single flower with minimal embellishment.

Left: *A single miniature calla features a natural stem to which a wired-and-taped leaf is added using a ribbon wrap that matches the spaghetti ribbon bow. Rhinestone sprays, inserted into the throat of the flower and held in place with floral adhesive, create upscale sparkle.*

Center: The ruby throat of a citrus-colored *Cymbidium* orchid is dramatized by the use of glittered ruby ribbon and coordinating Handy™ 5-stone Rhinestone Sprays. Italian *Ruscus* surrounds the flower, and a curled corsage stem adds the perfect feminine finish.

Right: *Small blue* Eryngium *blooms offer an unexpected textural contrast to the velvety rose in this versatile corsage. Italian* Ruscus *and a bow of satin-and-sheer ribbon provide comfortable surroundings while blue decorative wire spun over a deep blue ribbon stem wrap accentuates the cool color harmony.*

BOUTONNIÈRES

A flower and a leaf is all it takes to make a gentleman's boutonnière. But there are endless combinations of flowers, fillers and foliages to make these simple designs special. The mechanics of boutonnière making are the same as for corsages. Wire and tape provide the foundation, and floral adhesive can be employed to add lightweight accents or decorative embellishments. Because these finished designs are intended to be small, (typically 3-1/2 inches or less in height), the key is to control the proportions relative to the size and number of elements included. The examples shown here demonstrate classic and creative boutonnière combinations.

TOP	**Left:** *Rose, Italian* Ruscus *and* Eryngium, *with ribbon and decorative wire stem wrap.* **Center:** *Lily bud, button spray mums,* Hypericum *berries, pepperberry, plumosa fern and square-trimmed* Galax *leaves, with a stem wrap of OASIS™ Bind Wire.* **Right:** *A monochromatic combination of a carnation and a spray rose and spray rose bud, with willow* Eucalyptus *leaves.*
CENTER	**Left:** *Succulent,* Hypericum *berries, bonsai* Eucalyptus *and plumosa fern backed with a single salal leaf.* **Center:** *Petite* Ranunculus, *bonsai* Eucalyptus *and a single* Gerbera *center (with outer ray petals removed).* **Right:** *Miniature calla, Italian* Ruscus, *rhinestone sprays and a spaghetti ribbon wrap.*
BOTTOM	**Left:** *Standard carnation, a trio of baby's breath clusters and leatherleaf fern.* **Center:** Stephanotis, *green and variegated ivy, plumosa fern and iridescent OASIS™ Mega Beaded Wire beads.* **Right:** *Miniature* Gerbera, Craspedia *trio, salal leaf duo and an accent of waxflower.*

TIP TO TRY

HOW TO PIN A BOUTONNIÈRE

The impact of a handsome boutonnière is spoiled when poorly attached to the lapel. Use these tips to get it right.

- Position the boutonnière on the left lapel, just above the heart.
- The center of the design should sit about 4 to 4-1/2 inches below the shoulder.
- Begin pinning from the back of the lapel.
- Insert the pin through the fabric, then through the stem just beneath the flowers.
- Make a small stitch through the fabric on the opposite side of the stem.
- End with the tip of the pin on the back side of the lapel.
- If a second pin is needed to support the weight of the design, position it 1/2 inch higher than the first, stitching from the back, through the foliage or across the individual wired stems.

WRIST CORSAGES

The wrist corsage is a popular choice for proms, weddings and other special occasions. Wearing flowers on the wrist protects them from potential damage caused to shoulder corsages when hugging, dancing or wearing a coat. A wrist corsage must be well balanced so it sits comfortably on the forearm. The height should be limited to prevent a top-heaviness that can make the design floppy. For best results, choose small and lightweight flowers and greens such as those listed in the chart below.

FLOWERS	FILLERS	FOLIAGES
Alstroemeria	Baby's Breath	Boxwood
Button Spray Mums	*Bupleurum*	English Ivy
Delphinium	*Calycina (Thryptomene)*	*Eucalyptus gunnii*
Dendrobium Orchids	*Eryngium*	Bracelet Honey Myrtle
Freesia	*Genista*	Italian *Ruscus*
Mokara Orchids	*Hypericum*	Leatherleaf Fern
Spray Roses	*Limonium*	Ming Fern
Stephanotis	*Aster* 'Monte Cassino'	Plumosa Fern
Sweet Peas	Pepperberry	Seeded *Eucalyptus*
Sweetheart Roses	Waxflower	Silver Dollar *Eucalyptus*

GLUED WRIST CORSAGE

SUGGESTED MATERIALS:

Israeli *Ruscus*
Dusty Miller
Alstroemeria
Sweet Pea
Baby's Breath
No. 3 Sheer Ribbon
Rhinestone Sprays Double Row
Square-Stone Wristlet

Options abound for wristlets and decorative bracelets manufactured specifically for wrist corsages. These bases speed the design process by providing a foundation to which all of the design elements can be glued. The addition of ribbon provides color and a fluffy surface that establishes the design shape. Gems, jewels and other decorative accents are the finishing touches that provide texture, variety and sparkle.

DESIGN STEPS

Lay the wristlet on the table, with the square plastic platform face down. Clip Israeli *Ruscus* leaves in half, and use OASIS® Floral Adhesive to glue each half to the back of the platform, with the front side of each leaf facing the table.

Position the leaves in an overlapping pattern to completely cover the plastic.

Turn the wristlet right side up. The finished foliage outline should be a diamond or oval.

Glue a trio of small dusty miller leaves to the top of the plastic platform, with the stems radiating from the center outward.

Create a corsage bow using No. 3 ribbon. Apply a liberal amount of adhesive to the back center of the bow. Position the bow in the center of the platform, and allow the adhesive to set before moving to the next step.

Fluff the loops of the bow, then add three to five dusty miller leaves, gluing the base of each leaf deep among the loops.

DESIGN STEPS

Glue three *Alstroemeria* blooms into the bow, allowing space between each for other flower placements.

Add three to five individual sweet pea blossoms among the loops in the spaces between the *Alstroemeria* blooms.

Be sure the stems of all flowers are short so the blooms tuck closely into the bow.

Add small tufts of baby's breath intermingled with similarly sized clusters of rhinestone sprays.

The baby's breath and rhinestone sprays should fill the remaining gaps in the design.

Mokara orchids and rose-colored rhinestone sprays rest among sheer metallic ribbon on an Atlantic® Slaplet Wristlet in this elegantly modern monochromatic composition.

USING FLORAL ADHESIVE

OASIS® Floral Adhesive is the go-to glue for many flowers to wear. Sometimes referred to as "cold glue" or "liquid floral adhesive," this specially formulated adhesive is sold in tube form or a combination package with can and applicator bottle. When working with floral adhesive, follow these helpful tips:

- Dispense a small amount at a time.
- Create a puddle of glue for dipping stems.
- Apply glue to both the flower and the design surface for quick adhesion.
- A few seconds of air exposure makes the adhesive tacky and easier to work with for some applications.
- Allow glue to dry completely before storing in refrigeration.
- A dab of petroleum jelly on the tip of the tube or lid of the can will ease opening with future use.

A collection of wristlet styles await floral adornment. The ribbon ties, which hold the plastic platforms to the bases, will be covered when the flowers are added.

This lovely lineup of finished wristlets demonstrates the potential for versatile looks using similar materials.

A filigree cuff is a perfect backdrop for this botanical collection of spray roses, *Leucadendron*, and the centers of miniature *Gerbera*.

This rhinestone-studded wristlet contrasts nicely with the all white collection of roses, *Stephanotis* and beads from OASIS™ Mega Beaded Wire.

Rose-gold pearls and copper ribbon provide a coordinated base for this ensemble of *Stephanotis*, *Ranunculus* and *Eucalyptus gunnii*.

Sweetheart roses, metallic ribbon, gold rhinestone sprays and a rhinestone wristlet provide the feeling of formal elegance.

A double-strand pearl wristlet holds a monochromatic gathering of violet *Alstroemeria* and waxflower.

HAIR FLOWERS

Flowers worn in the hair for special occasions present some unique requirements. Designs must generally be small and lightweight. Styling must be relatively flat and curved to conform to the shape of the head. Attachment methods must be considered, and different hair types and colors must be accommodated. Mechanics often involve a combination of wire and glue. The best flower options, typically petite blossoms or delicate fillers, mirror those for wrist corsages. Refer to the chart in the previous section for recommended fresh materials.

SIMPLE HAIR CLIP

Small floral accents for the hair can be made quite simply with a leaf base to which fresh flowers and fillers are glued. The wire ends, hidden beneath the leaves, become the attachment method using common hairpins. If a client prefers a hair comb, no wire is needed. The same design can be glued to the plastic comb.

Wire and tape three ivy leaves. Stack two of the leaves face-to-face, then add the third leaf behind either one.

Line up the leaves so the bases are even, and tape the three leaves into a single unit. Wrap the tape over itself but not further down the trio of wires.

DESIGN STEPS

Trim the taped wire stems to about an inch or less. Bend each individual wire end backward, each forming a "U" shape. With the wire stem positioned horizontally, bend backward to 180 degrees the single leaf that faces the opposite of the other two. Here the bending of this leaf is shown in progress, not yet complete.

Once completely bent to 180 degrees, the leaf should hide the wire ends. Hold the single leaf and wire stem, and spread apart the other two leaves, shaping the trio into a flat formation.

Use OASIS® Floral Adhesive to create a base of filler flowers such as the waxflower used here.

Glue a single orchid or other focal flower into the center.

Adjust the fillers as needed to unify the elements.

This view from beneath shows the horizontal position of the wire stem used to pin the design into the hair. ***Note:*** Limited depth and an arching shape ensure the finished hairpiece sits comfortably against the head.

HAIR CLUSTER

When a larger hair accent is desired, a cluster of flowers can be designed using wire to create an arch or band. As the size of the hairpiece increases, the designer must be careful to control the weight of the design. Here, lightweight plumosa fern and baby's breath are used to create a crescent-shaped cluster suitable to be worn in a variety of positions on the side of the head or in back.

1. Bend an 18-inch 22-gauge wire to form a narrow pointed oval. Twist the ends of the wires around each other to secure.

2. Stack together two or three small pieces of plumosa fern, and position them with the tips extending slightly beyond the end of the oval. Use 28- or 30-gauge wire, paddle wire or bullion wire to wrap the wire frame multiple times, securing the plumosa to the base.

3. Repeat step 2 on the opposite end of the wire frame. Fill in the center with additional plumosa fern, as needed. If using 18-inch florist wire, multiple pieces will be needed to secure the greens. For paddle wire or bullion, a continuous wire can be used for all attachments.

4. Add baby's breath to the foliage base, securing it with floral adhesive. A very light application of adhesive will hold the petite flower clusters in place. The finished design can then be shaped as desired.

FLORAL HALO

The floral halo is a classic floral accessory for the hair. Also called a circlet or floral wreath, this style is popular for brides, bridesmaids and flower girls. In the English tradition, the halo is often designed with large, full blossoms assembled with whimsical irregularity. On the opposite end of the spectrum, halos are sometimes delicate and minimal, perhaps with nothing more than ivy and a few accent flowers. Here is demonstrated something in between – fully flowered, yet uniform in shape and lightweight in appearance.

SUGGESTED MATERIALS:

Spray Roses

Alstroemeria

Plumosa Fern

Seeded *Eucalyptus*

Seafoam Statice

DESIGN STEPS

Use two or three 18-gauge wires to form the desired size circular frame. For correct sizing, use a piece of ribbon to measure the wearer's head where the halo will be worn – either across the forehead or on the crown of the head. Twist the wires around each other or tape them to secure the ring. Cluster two or three stems of plumosa fern together, and align them along the wire frame. Bind then into place with 28- or 30-gauge paddle wire. Repeat, overlapping stems of plumosa until the wire ring is covered.

Use OASIS® Floral Adhesive to dot the wreath with small clusters of seeded *Eucalyptus*, using both the seeds and the leaves to provide contrast against the plumosa fern.

Glue six or seven spray roses around the frame, using rhythmic yet irregular spacing and varied flower facings, with some facing upward and others outward or downward. Add pieces of seafoam statice in varied sizes around the wreath to complement the roses.

Add three or four *Alstroemeria* blooms between the spray roses to unify the circular rhythm. Add more seafoam statice, as needed, to balance the colors. Use No. 3 sheer ribbon to complete the circle, tucking and gluing it into looped positions among the flowers.

The completed halo pairs nicely with the flower girl pomander demonstrated on Pages 251-253.

Chapter Six

WEDDING BOUQUETS

Wedding flowers are a special niche that require precision and finesse as well as an eye for color and texture, space and balance. Bouquets are the cream among wedding floral designs. Great care is necessary to achieve professional results worthy of a bride's special day. Though trends in wedding bouquets shift along with fashion and decorating trends, key design shapes never really go out of style. In this chapter, classical design outlines are paired with current floral favorites to demonstrate a wealth of possibilities for the bridal client. By modifying the color combinations and flower recipes of the step-by-step styles and their accompanying bouquet variations, hundreds of options are possible.

BIEDERMEIER BOUQUET

Biedermeier is a variation of the classic round bouquet style. Instead of a scattered flower combination, its defining characteristic is the use of flowers to form concentric rings of color. Flowers and foliage are selected to provide not only color variation from one ring to the next but also variation in flower form and texture.

In this style, close flower placement is necessary to achieve the compact shape and clearly patterned rows that give the bouquet its distinctive appearance. Though it can be made in a bouquet holder with either a straight or slanted handle, the straight handle presents the flowers in a more modern way reminiscent of a hand-tied bouquet. An added advantage of this format is the ability to check the rounded form and ring patterns from a birds-eye view while designing.

SUGGESTED MATERIALS:

- Roses
- Larkspur
- *Alstroemeria* or *Stephanotis*
- Spray (Miniature) Carnations
- Button Spray (Pompon) Chrysanthemums
- *Hypericum*
- *Limonium sinensis*

DESIGN STEPS

Use six to eight stems of larkspur or other line flowers to create a circular outline at the base of the bouquet holder. Placements should be horizontal, with each stem the same length. Strive for consistent spacing, like spokes on a wheel. Add a single rose or other upright focal flower in the center of the foam. The tip of the rose should extend to about four inches above the foam in bouquet holder.

Surround the rose with tightly clustered stems of *Limonium sinensis* or a similar filler such as baby's breath or *Thryptomene calycina*. The *Limonium* should cover the lower half of the rose. Use additional larkspur to fill in the spaces between the initial larkspur "spokes." Larkspur buds and lower stem segments can be paired with the tips to create volume.

Use button spray mums to create a continuous ring above the larkspur. Stems should all be the same length, about an inch shorter than the larkspur. Strive for blooms of a consistent size, or create a pattern varying larger and smaller blooms around the ring. Add a second ring of button mums surrounding the ring of *Limonium*. Make this ring different by allowing even spaces between the button mum blooms.

Add spray (miniature) carnations between the button mums to complete the upper ring. Add tight clusters of *Limonium* to form a continuous ring above the lower ring of button mums. Make sure these clusters are slightly shorter than the button mums so that a mounded form begins to develop from edge to top.

Add a solid ring of spray carnations above the *Limonium*. Stems should be slightly shorter than the *Limonium* to continue the gradual mounding. Fluff open the blooms as needed to achieve a consistent flower size. Arrange the spray carnations close together so there are no gaps between them, but avoid crowding the flowers so they maintain their round form.

Fill in the remaining space between the upper and lower rings with *Hypericum*. Cluster the berries close together so the bouquet holder is hidden. If the space is wide, use another flower or foliage, or even reindeer moss, to create an additional row.

If desired, add *Stephanotis* or *Alstroemeria* blooms intermittently within or between rows to add impact. *Stephanotis* can be inserted on wires or Stemsons® Stay Fresh® Stephanotis Stems. *Alstroemeria* blooms can be inserted on their natural stems (if long enough) or glued in with OASIS® Floral Adhesive.

The finished bouquet can be enhanced with beads or gems. Here, a second row of *Stephanotis* is added, each bloom embellished with a clear LOMEY™ Diamante Pin inserted in the center.

Alstroemeria and beads from OASIS™ MEGA Beaded Wire are used to give this Biedermeier-style bouquet a more subtle, romantic look.

A cluster of white tulips takes the place of the central rose, and *Hydrangea* and waxflower clusters form the outer edge of this springtime Biedermeier bouquet. OASIS™ 2-inch Floral Lace, attached with OASIS® UGLU™ Adhesive Strips, makes a lovely coordinating handle wrap.

HAND-TIED BOUQUET

The hand-tied bouquet is a popular choice for both brides and bridesmaids. Designed as a clutch or handful of flowers with natural stems forming the handle, this style has the versatility to be formal or casual, dense or airy, glamorous or whimsical. Generally round in form, the outline can be loosely defined or highly irregular. Cascading variations are also possible.

SUGGESTED MATERIALS:

Roses
Standard Carnations
Aster ericoides 'Monte Cassino'
Aster novi-belgii
Hypericum
Dusty Miller
Israeli *Ruscus*
Salal
No. 9 Sheer or Satin Ribbon

Though construction techniques vary among designers, most rely on a framework of filler and/or foliage to support the positioning of the featured floral elements. Here, a spindled-stem method is used. Beginners may prefer a hybrid approach involving both spiraling and lacing of stems so that preliminary and final stem placements are angled in the same direction as the handle develops while other stems are threaded through the center and held in place by the interlocking stems.

DESIGN STEPS

Prepare all flowers and foliage by stripping the leaves and thorns off the lower two-thirds of each stem. Begin with two stems, a focal flower such as a rose and a filler or foliage, and position them next to each other with stems angling in opposite direction (forming an "X"). Hold the stems together about 3 to 4 inches from the top with one hand. Avoid gripping the flowers with a fist because this will bunch them together rather than giving each one space.

Rotate the stems slightly, and add another focal flower and filler, making sure stems are angled as much as 45 degrees. Rotate and repeat again, forming a center with three focal flowers. Keep the grip relaxed, with fingers as open as possible, so flowers remain well-spaced. Rotating the bouquet and adding each flower from the same side achieves a spiraled-stem finish. Here, the designer positions each flower head to the left and the stem to the right.

Add a secondary flower, such as carnation, to the edge of the bouquet, in the space between two of the roses. Repeat with two more carnations positioned similarly near the other rose pairs. When properly placed, these three flowers will be spread equally around the outside edges of the bouquet. Supplement each of these placements with a stem of filler or foliage.

Begin developing a rounded exterior using flowers, fillers and foliage. Rotate the bouquet, as needed, to develop every side. Continue to angle stems and add them from the same direction so they flare apart from one another below the grip.

Use foliage to refine the edges of the bouquet and fill gaps. As needed, gently lift any center flowers that may have sunk in order to achieve a pleasant rise and fall among the blooms. Be sure the focal flowers are emphasized, and make any final adjustments including removing and repositioning stems that may have become crowded.

Use self-fusing OASIS™ BIND-IT™ Tape to secure the stems where they have been gripped (the binding point). To do so, cut a piece approximately 8 to 9 inches, and remove the plastic backing. Hold the end of the tape against the bouquet stems, and wrap while stretching until the entire piece is used and the tape sticks to itself. Trim the flower stems to the desired length.

Use No. 9 sheer or satin ribbon to cover the binding and extend down several inches of the stems, to create a comfortable handle. Use clusters of pearl-headed corsage or boutonnière pins to add a decorative touch. Angle the pins as parallel to the flower stems as possible so they do not poke through the opposite side of the stem bundle.

Place the finished bouquet into a vase containing 2 to 3 inches of properly mixed flower food solution, and store in the floral cooler.

This monobotanical hand-tied bouquet allows a dozen roses to take the starring role, with white *Genista* and *Eucalyptus gunnii* radiating freely at the edges.

This gardeny gathering takes an opposite approach, using one-of-this and one-of-that to achieve a whimsical flower mix within a well-defined circular form.

This meadow-inspired mix uses numerous filler flowers and limited focal flowers to create a loosely arching bouquet that feels less structured and more free-spirited.

Analogous colors of yellow, lime and blue blend comfortably in this open rounded mass hand-tied bouquet. Flowers are used in twos and threes to achieve pleasant unity throughout the design.

SUGGESTED MATERIALS:
Roses
Miniature Spray Chrysanthemums
Limonium
Italian *Ruscus*
Salal
Eucalyptus gunnii

PRESENTATION BOUQUET

The presentation bouquet is a sophisticated variation of the hand-tied style. Also known as an arm bouquet, the presentation bouquet is the classic bouquet style presented in honor of an award, a performance, graduation or similar special occasion. More elongated and one-sided than the typical round hand-tied, the presentation bouquet has an air of regal elegance as it is carried horizontally on the bride's forearm.

This style welcomes many flower combinations, from classic roses to garden favorites such as *Delphinium* and tulips. Elegant wedding mixes, including peonies, *Ranunculus*, *Anemone*, *Freesia*, orchids and callas, also meld easily into this bouquet style. An armful of meadow-like flowers, such as larkspur, *Aster*, *Boronia*, *Solidago*, *Limonium*, *Gypsophila* and *Zinnia*, is well-suited to informal outdoor weddings. Though the presentation bouquet is often designed in the hand, here it is constructed on a tabletop, which is often easier for beginners and more efficient when designing in multiples.

DESIGN STEPS

Clean the lower half of all stems. Depending on their position, some stems may need to have additional greens and thorns removed. Position two to three pieces of Italian *Ruscus* on the tabletop so they are aligned with tips similar in height and stems angled toward each other.

Center the first rose about 3 to 4 inches below the tips of the *Ruscus*. Position a second rose below the first and to the right or left. Add one or two stems of salal below the rose stems, allowing them to angle away from the center line to begin broadening the bouquet shape.

Add a third rose to the opposite side and a step lower than the second. Partner another rose directly across the center line from this one. As the outer flowers and greens are added, angle the stem ends toward the center.

Add a center rose a step below the previous pair, and flank this rose with two others, increasing the bouquet width and stem angles slightly. If needed, add more foliage to provide lift to the central flowers.

Begin adding stems of miniature spray chrysanthemums, starting near the top of the bouquet. Carefully thread each stem through the network of rose stems and greens.

Progress from tip to base in a stairstepped manner, placing the miniature spray mums in the spaces between the rose stems.

Add stems of miniature spray mums to support the positions of the outermost rose stems at the base of the bouquet.

Soften the bouquet with stems of *Limonium* and *Eucalyptus gunnii*, following a similar progression of insertions from tip to base. Make sure the fillers are used to complete the sides of the bouquet as well as the top.

Add salal to cover the flower stems beneath the lowest flowers. Gather the stems to form a binding point 3 to 4 inches below the bottom-most flowers, and secure with floral tape or OASIS™ BIND-IT™ Tape.

Trim the stems into a neat unit approximately one-third the total length of the bouquet. Add a ribbon accent to cover the binding point. Here, OASIS™ Sequin Wrap is tied in a simple knot. For added grandeur, a multiloop bow could also be used.

Hold the finished bouquet in its intended position on your forearm, and make adjustments, as needed, to showcase the individual flowers.

Callas have a stately elegance that is showcased nicely in the presentation bouquet style. Here, miniature callas make a simple statement, with a light touch of greens and a modern wrap of OASIS™ 2-inch Raw Jute and OASIS™ 1-inch Flat Wire.

This garden-inspired presentation bouquet capitalizes on the natural arch of the *Dendrobium* orchids and hyacinths to create a subtle crescent form. Designed with groupings of individual flower types, the larkspur and *Liatris* serve to extend the line while roses enhance the feeling of abundance.

Gerbera hold their own among a bold collection of foliages. OASIS™ 2-inch Raw Jute ribbon works well to create a bow that enhances but does not compete with the flowers.

HOW TO HOLD A BOUQUET

Brides and bridesmaids generally have limited experience carrying bouquets of flowers. Take the opportunity to educate them on proper carriage of wedding flowers by sharing these pointers.

- For the processional, recessional and formal wedding photos, hold the bouquet so it is centered in front of the body. Use two hands to grip the bouquet, keeping hands just below the navel and arms comfortably bent.
- Keep the bouquet upright. A well-balanced bouquet should not tip forward. Avoid holding the bouquet with arms in an upright "praying" position.
- Hold presentation bouquets on one arm, gently cradling the flowers like a baby.
- Hold pomanders in front of the body using two hands, palms up, one on top of another.
- Hold a scepter or wand on an angle with two hands, one gripping the bouquet near the binding point and the other hand supporting a lower portion of the stem.

CASCADE BOUQUET

Cascade bouquets are the grand bouquets of the past and the new bouquets of the present. After several years out of the spotlight, the cascade style has seen a resurgence among brides who want something more spectacular or more original than the popular hand-tied bouquet.

The classic cascade bouquet is long and flowing, with considerable volume and a strong central focal point. While shapes may vary from slim to broad, and lengths may vary from a trickle to a waterfall, these bouquets have in common the drama of cascading lines created by flowers, fillers, foliages, and sometimes ribbons and other flowing accessories.

SUGGESTED MATERIALS:

Larkspur

Tulips

Freesia

Miniature Spray Chrysanthemums

Heather

Leatherleaf Fern

Willow-leaf *Eucalyptus*

DESIGN STEPS

Green up a slant-handled Extra-large LOMEY® Bouquet Holder using leatherleaf fern to establish a tapered outline that is rounded at the top and pointed at the bottom. Use willow-leaf *Eucalyptus* to supplement and extend the outline.

Lightly fill in the center of the bouquet holder with additional leatherleaf and *Eucalyptus*. Then place larkspur to create an extended line out of the bottom of the bouquet holder. Place three or four additional larkspurs in a stairstepped manner, each increasingly shorter, on the lower left side of the bouquet. Complement this group with three or four larkspurs radiating from the upper right side of the holder.

Insert a tulip into the bottom of the bouquet holder so it extends midway into the cascade, with a clear downward flow. Add a second tulip in the gap between the cascading tulip and the larkspur on the upper right. Position a second tulip pair in the upper left quadrant to finish the tapered bouquet outline.

Establish the focal area in the center of the bouquet holder using three tulips positioned to form a triangle. Allow space between the tulips, and vary the flower facings so the top flower faces upward and the others angle slightly toward the sides.

Arrange *Freesia* to fill out the bouquet form, positioning them first throughout the focal area and increasing the spacing as you add them at the bouquet edges. Allow the *Freesia* in the center to extend slightly beyond the tulips, to develop a feeling of depth and create a mounded center.

Add linear stems of heather to enhance the bouquet and unify the tulips and *Freesia*. Begin with shorter stems inserted in the center so they radiate outward, then add longer stems at the edges, finishing with the longest stems flowing into the cascade.

Clip stems of miniature spray mums into segments with two to three flowers each, and arrange them among the central flowers to fill gaps and enhance the shape. Extend a few additional miniature mums into the cascade to help unify it with the top.

VARIATIONS

Linear *Dendrobium* orchids create the outline, and *Cymbidium* orchids provide the focal emphasis in this uncomplicated cascade variation. Mixed foliages, including plumosa fern, *Aspidistra*, *Ruscus*, *Eucalyptus* and lily grass add variety, enhance texture and exaggerate the cascading lines.

The open form of this cascade bouquet is achieved by first designing a teardrop-shaped core, then using lily grass, callas and seeded *Eucalyptus* to expand the outline. Negative space gives the individual flowers greater impact and enhances the modern styling.

The crescent bouquet is a variation of the cascade style in which the cascade flows to the side rather than down the center. Often in this style, the rule of thirds is used to create a nicely proportioned design in which the long end of the bouquet, when measured from the center to the tip, is equal to two-thirds of the total bouquet length and the short end is one-third of the total length. A straight-handled bouquet holder, such as the OASIS® Wedding Belle® Holders, allows development of volume in the center. Linear materials with natural arching lines, such as Italian *Ruscus,* heather and *Genista*, enhance the desired curved outline. With this style, it is important to vary the flower facings so the central flowers face forward, transitioning to more angled and downward facings on each end.

SUGGESTED MATERIALS:

Roses

Spray Roses

Standard Carnations

Stock

21" LOMEY® Pedestal

OASIS™ Metallic Wire (Silver)

OASIS™ Beaded Wire (Iridescent)

OASIS™ MEGA Beaded Wire (White and Iridescent)

IGLU® Holder

OASIS® UGLU™ Adhesive Strips

OASIS® Floral Adhesive

SCEPTER BOUQUET

The scepter is a regal bouquet option for the bride seeking something creative for herself, her bridesmaids or even young flower girls. Typically, this decorative staff is capped with a cluster or ball of flowers. The addition of flowing ribbons announces the bride's grand entrance when carried by enthusiastic flower girls.

Mechanics for this bouquet style run the gamut from curtain rods to wood dowels. Here, a LOMEY® Pedestal provides the perfect foundation, thanks to its light weight, sturdy stem and solid plastic platform.

An IGLU® Holder is secured to the top of the pedestal with OASIS® Floral Adhesive, after the stem is wrapped with a combination of metallic and beaded wires. Clear OASIS® UGLU™ Adhesive Strips applied to the upper half of the pedestal before wrapping help prevent the decorative wires from slipping.

Short-stemmed roses and carnations effectively fill the IGLU® Holder to form a rounded top. Stems of stocks, cut into segments, fill the gaps, and spray roses add dimension. Floral Adhesive is used to dot beads from OASIS™ MEGA Beaded Wire throughout the design in singles, pairs and trios, achieving unity with the beaded handle.

BOUQUET HOLDER MECHANICS

Floral foam bouquet holders allow florists to quickly design a variety of bouquet shapes. They provide the added advantage of a water source to keep the flowers fresh. Basic styles are typically made of white or clear plastic, they are easily manipulated for a variety of uses or effects.

VARIATIONS

This *Alstroemeria* scepter, or wand, bouquet is created by stripping the lower foliage and clustering the blooms into a rounded mass. The stems are tightly bound first with OASIS™ Bullion Wire in a random crisscross pattern, then with wraps of OASIS™ Diamond Wire at the top and near the base. Clear OASIS™ BIND-IT™ Tape can be used to secure the stems at the top and base before the decorative wire is applied.

The clean stems of callas make them an ideal flower for use in scepter, or wand, bouquets. Using six to eight stems, with blooms clustered together, this design is quick to assemble, using OASIS® UGLU™ Adhesive Strips to secure the OASIS™ Sequin Wrap and a few twists of OASIS™ Beaded Wire that bind the stems.

A. Salal leaves are glued to the back of this straight-handled OASIS® Grande Wedding Belle® Holder. To do so, the stem is removed from each leaf, and a hole punch is used to create a perfect opening for the bouquet handle to be inserted through each leaf. OASIS® Floral Adhesive on the backs of the leaves further holds them in the desired overlapping position. The plastic handle is then enrobed in OASIS™ Sequin Wrap followed by a crisscrossed embellishment of OASIS™ Iridescent Beaded Wire.

B. An OASIS® Grande Wedding Belle® Holder receives added support from a cage of OASIS™ Florist Netting (chicken wire) carefully formed over the top of the bouquet holder's floral foam cage. Space between the floral foam cage and the florist netting cage ensures that stems can be inserted easily into the foam. The back of the bouquet holder must be finished with foliage or ribbon to cover the florist-netting mechanic.

C. An OASIS® Large Wedding Belle® Holder with a slant handle is transformed into a faux hand-tied handle by securing a bundle of flower stems to the handle with OASIS® UGLU™ Adhesive Strips and binding with Floratape® Stem Wrap. *Galax* leaves are glued in an overlapping manner to cover the base of the holder, and a wrap of OASIS™ Raw Jute provides a decorative covering where the stems and leaves meet. Boutonnière pins clustered in pairs and trios secure the wrap and add a pleasing finishing touch.

COMPOSITE FLOWER BOUQUET

A composite flower is a man-made assemblage of flower petals resulting in an oversized "fantasy" version of a botanical specimen. The "glamellia" is the classic composite flower, designed with Gladiolus *blossoms to resemble a fully open* Camellia. *The "duchess rose" is similarly luxurious, with an open rose surrounded by abundant rows of rose petals.*

Small composite flowers are sometimes used in corsages. Today, oversized versions are popular as bouquets. They can also be used effectively as pew decorations, cake toppers and accents to many ceremony and reception decorations.

SUGGESTED MATERIALS:

Roses

Salal

OASIS® Floral Adhesive

Floratape® Stem Wrap

22-Gauge OASIS™ Florist Wire

No. 9 Ribbon

Cardboard Flange from a Ribbon Spool

DESIGN STEPS

Apply a liberal layer of OASIS® Floral Adhesive to a cardboard circle from a ribbon roll. (Alternatively, use a vase as a stencil to cut a circle from a cardboard rose box.) Dismantle a rose by separating the petals from the stem. Grip the flower from the top, and bend the bloom one direction and the stem the opposite direction until the petals release.

Use a florist knife to make a small slice in the center of the base of several rose petals, and apply the petals to the glue-covered cardboard ring. The slice in the petals helps ensure they lay flat, thus hiding the cardboard beneath and providing the appearance that the fantasy bloom is fully open. Make sure each petal extends past the cardboard edge. Petals should overlap one another, creating a scalloped effect.

After the first ring is complete, apply floral adhesive to the bases of the outsides of the petals. Then, create a second row of petals, continuing to slice the base of each petal. Position the petals a bit closer to the center opening of the cardboard ring, with the tip of each petal falling in the space between the petals it overlaps.

Continue gluing rows of petals in a similar fashion. After two or three rows, the petals should no longer be sliced because their naturally curved shape will add lift, body and dimension to the center of the developing composition.

When the cardboard ring is completely covered, a cup-like center will be formed. Check the composition from all sides, and glue in additional petals, as needed, to fill any gaps and/or hide any visible cardboard.

Select a well-formed open rose, and trim the stem to about 1½ inches. Use two 20-gauge wires to cross-pierce the rose's calyx, and bend the wires downward, parallel to the rose stem. Insert the wires through the hole in the middle of the cardboard, and pull the rose into the center cup of petals.

Use 22-gauge wire to stitch wire several salal leaves, and then tape each wire stem. Apply the leaves to the base of the cardboard circle in an overlapping manner, bending them horizontally to support the collar, with the front of each leaf facing the cardboard. Tape the wired-and-taped leaf stems to the wire extending from the center rose with stem wrap/floral tape, to create a handle for the bouquet.

Add a second row of salal leaves, reversing this row so the front of each leaf faces the back of the bouquet. Secure with stem wrap/floral tape.

Trim the individual wires to the desired handle length, then tape all of the wires into a single unit.

Wrap the handle with No. 9 ribbon, and tie on a bow or streamers if desired.

This duchess rose variation is created by extending the wire handle with additional pieces of florist wire, varying the lengths so the finished stem is tapered. Tape the wire stem, then add wired salal leaves. Finish by shaping the stem to add graceful curvature.

POMANDER BOUQUET

SUGGESTED MATERIALS:

Mokara Orchids

Spray Roses

Bells-of-Ireland

Hypericum

Seeded *Eucalyptus*

The pomander is a spherical bouquet suspended from a looped handle. Also known as a kissing ball, this design is often covered completely with flowers or flower petals. Pomanders are easily accomplished using OASIS® Floral Foam Spheres. By using different sphere sizes and varying the loop length, the pomander can be designed to suit the bride, bridesmaids or flower girls.

DESIGN STEPS

Insert a plastic drinking straw through the center of a soaked OASIS® Floral Foam Sphere. Use a straw with an opening large enough for a hyacinth stake to slide through.

Insert a hyacinth stake through the straw to push out the foam plug, then remove the hyacinth stake. Cut a piece of No. 9 double-face satin ribbon approximately 30 to 34 inches long. Fold the ribbon in half, and use the hyacinth stake to push the looped end of the ribbon through the straw.

When the ribbon emerges, hold onto the loop while pulling the hyacinth stake back out of the straw.

Pull the ribbon further through the straw to achieve a loop of the desired size for carrying or hanging the pomander. Tie the lower ends of the ribbon into a knot, catching a stem or wood pick in the knot to prevent the ribbon from pulling through the straw.

Cut bells-of-Ireland into segments by snipping just above each cluster of green "bells." Discard the small soft tip segment. Insert the segments into the foam sphere, beginning at the top, so the flowers are flush with the foam.

Continue adding segments of bells-of-Ireland to completely cover the sphere. Nestle the flowers close to one another so an even shape is achieved and the foam is hidden.

Create three or four small double-loop bows using ribbon that matches the handle. Insert the wires of each bow through the bells-of-Ireland and into the sphere so they surround the handle. Add spray roses and *Hypericum* among the ribbon loops.

Add seeded *Eucalyptus* for texture, and use floral adhesive to glue *Mokara* orchids, as desired, onto the upper half of the sphere.

An unconventional ring-bearer design (right) pairs nicely with this citrus-colored pomander for a flower girl.

An OASIS® Square European Bouquet Holder makes a creative floral alternative to the traditional ring pillow.

RIBBON POMANDER VARIATION

This pomander variation uses clusters of ribbon bows to create the sphere into which floral materials are glued. The result is a petite, lightweight and sturdy pomander suitable for carrying by even the youngest flower girl.

SUGGESTED MATERIALS:

Spray Roses
Alstroemeria
Seafoam Statice
Seeded *Eucalyptus*
Plumosa Fern
No. 3 Sheer Wired Ribbon

DESIGN STEPS

Use No. 3 sheer wired ribbon to make eight corsage bows of equal size. Secure each bow with 24-gauge OASIS™ Florist Wire.

Gather the bows into a group. Align the wires from each bow, and twist them together to form a single unit. Form the unit of twisted stems into a small loop.

Tie a length of matching ribbon to the wire loop, to form a handle. Then, begin gluing floral materials among the loops. Start with small clusters of seeded *Eucalyptus* followed by tips of plumosa fern.

Clip seafoam statice into individual tufts, and glue them into the ribbon. Position the statice evenly among the loops to achieve a nicely rounded shape.

Cut the stems of the spray roses to about ½ inch in length, apply OASIS® Floral Adhesive to the base of each flower and glue into the ribbon ball. Vary the flower facings so each radiates outward.

Completely remove the stem of each *Alstroemeria*, apply floral adhesive to the base of the petals and glue into the design, to complete the rounded form.

The finished pomander makes a sweet companion to the flower girl halo demonstrated in Chapter 5, pages 204-207.

Floral design by Kevin Ylvisaker AIFD, PFCI

Chapter Seven

SYMPATHY FLOWERS

Flowers have long been a preferred means of expressing sympathy. Though modern funeral customs have shifted, flowers remain a meaningful way for family, friends, neighbors and business associates to express sorrow and mourn a loss. Today's sympathy tributes are sometimes smaller and fewer than in the past, but what hasn't changed is the sense of warmth and comfort that these arrangements contribute to the funeral setting.

Sympathy design styles include casket sprays; easel designs; and arrangements in baskets, vases and urns. Simple tributes are sometimes comparable to everyday arrangements but may be given a religious or sorrowful tone through the colors or accessories used. Larger pieces sometimes involve specialized foundations or other design-specific mechanics. Here, instructions are provided for the major styles of sympathy designs.

TRADITIONAL SYMPATHY BASKET

Flowers designed in a basket or an urn are a commonly requested sympathy tribute. Most often these arrangements are designed with a triangular outline, including a tall central line providing stature and impact when viewed from a distance in a large church or funeral home setting. Sometimes the outermost points are connected with an arc of flowers creating a showy fan-like shape.

Despite their name, sympathy baskets are often designed in a number of container types other than baskets, including urns, vases, bowls and compotes. Plastic baskets are frequently used instead of wicker due to their ease of preparation and water holding capacity. Deluxe floral foam, which is more dense than standard foam, is ideal for large sprays of thick-stemmed flowers. When necessary, chicken wire can also be taped atop the foam to provide support for flower placements.

SUGGESTED MATERIALS:

Roses
Gladiolus
Stock
Heather
Flat Fern
Leatherleaf Fern
Salal
Eucalyptus gunnii

1.

Prepare the container with OASIS® Deluxe Floral Foam Maxlife to a height slightly above the rim. Secure with OASIS® Waterproof Tape, then begin creating a triangular outline with flat fern, beginning with points at the top and sides and then filling in between. *(See steps for greening up symmetrical triangle arrangements in Chapter 3.)* Add leatherleaf fern to fill gaps and enhance the radial rhythm of the stems, then add *Eucalyptus gunnii* for a bit of texture.

2.

Position a tall stem of *Gladiolus* vertically near the back center of the container. Add two slightly shorter *Gladiolus* to each side of the first to create a unified trio. Add a horizontal *Gladiolus* on each side of the container to establish the width of the design. Partner a second *Gladiolus* above each. Position a pair of *Gladiolus* in each of the two spaces between the top and sides of the design. Insert the *Gladiolus* deep into the foam to ensure they are stable.

3.

Use stock to create a line through the middle of the design, starting just below the *Gladiolus* trio and moving toward the front container edge in a stairstepped manner. Allow the spacing between the stock to widen as the placements progress to the base. Change the angles of the stems also so the lower flowers extend forward. Use two more stock on each side of this central line to unify with the horizontal *Gladiolus*.

4.

Use heather to fill out the shape, emphasizing taller linear pieces at the top and edges and shorter branched pieces in the center. Position the stems to provide strong radial rhythm from the center outward in all directions.

5.

Enhance the center of the design with roses, starting near the top and transitioning to the base. Be sure to shift the flower facings as they progress toward the container edge so the top roses face upward and the lowest roses face forward. Allow a couple of the stems to rest deep within the center to achieve a sense of depth.

This modernization of the traditional sympathy basket uses *Gladiolus* to form a central spire and Italian *Ruscus* to define the outer points of an implied triangle. Flowers and foliages are grouped for impact, with an offset trio of *Anthurium* counterbalanced by roses and *Genista*. A central bow of OASIS™ Raw Jute complements the papier-mâché container. Curly willow surrounds and extends the center of the design for added height and impact.

This exuberant design strikes the perfect balance between somber and celebratory for a modern celebration-of-life service. Spiral *Eucalyptus* radiates widely from the ECOssentials Cylinder, creating a stately background for the spirited display of *Gerbera*, *Hypericum* and 'Green Trick' *Dianthus*. Loops of OASIS™ 1" Flat Wire provide a modern edge. The bold color harmony is enhanced by the repetition of black *Gerbera* centers with the black container and the silver decorative wire with the gray *Eucalyptus*.

This traditional sympathy basket of roses and carnations stretches the proportions well beyond the basket handle, increasing not only the finished size but also the perceived value. The monochromatic color harmony reduces the number of flowers needed to achieve a unified composition. 'Green Trick' *Dianthus* and *Eucalyptus gunnii* remain neutral to the color palette but provide pleasing depth and texture. Crowning the design is emerald palm clipped nearly to the spine, which creates a prominent wreath-like accent to soften the appearance of the plastic basket handle.

CASKET SPRAYS

SUGGESTED MATERIALS:

Fuji Chrysanthemums

Oriental Lilies

Larkspur

Hydrangea

Stock

Aster ericoides 'Monte Cassino'

Limonium 'Misty Blue'

Eryngium

Emerald Palm

Salal

Silver Dollar *Eucalyptus*

Casket flowers should be ordered exclusively by the family of the deceased. Flowers designed for use on a casket will vary in size and sometimes in shape, depending on whether the casket will be half open, fully open or closed. A half-couch spray is typically designed for a half-open casket and is positioned on the closed foot end. A full-couch spray is designed for a closed casket and is placed in the center of the casket. A lid spray is designed for a fully open casket and is displayed above the open lid. A casket blanket is a solid surface of flowers generally designed on a fabric base to drape the entire casket. Casket scarves and garlands are smaller design options for clients who wish to make a simpler statement. Here, instructions for making the most common casket sprays, the full couch and half couch, are provided.

The full-couch casket spray is typically a symmetrical design in an oval shape. The design should cover two-thirds of the length of the casket, or more. Tapered from one end to the other, there should be a gentle swell and a clear focal point in the center. Frequently, the full couch is designed as a monobotanical composition, meaning it is made with a single flower type, such as roses or carnations. Here, a mixed composition is shown to demonstrate the proper succession of flower placements leading to a unified whole.

DESIGN STEPS

Prepare an OASIS™ Double Casket Saddle with two blocks of soaked OASIS® Deluxe Floral Foam Maxlife. Bevel the edges of the floral foam bricks to eliminate the square corners. Use OASIS® Waterproof Tape to secure the bricks in place.

Use emerald palm to create an elongated oval outline following the same process as described for the oblong centerpiece in Chapter 3. Greens should extend 15 to 18 inches from the ends of the saddle and 9 to 12 inches from the front and back sides. Angle the first placements downward so they are flush with the tabletop. This will ensure the finished design melds with the curved top of the casket.

Add stems of salal, radiating from the center outward, to fill gaps and complete the mounded silhouette. Then, add silver dollar *Eucalyptus* as needed to enhance color contrast and texture. The *Eucalyptus* stems should extend slightly beyond the outline of the other greens.

Begin the flower placements with larkspur extending just beyond the greens on the ends and along the sides. Use one or two flowers, plus additional buds, for each placement, leaving several inches of space between groups. From a birds-eye view, the larkspur should form a pointed oval shape. Add larkspur to the midsection of the spray, continuing to radiate stems from the center outward. Finish with a few larkspur flowers and/or buds extending from the top of the floral foam just beyond the greens.

Establish weight in the central focal area of the spray by placing three or four *Hydrangea* in a zigzag line from the front edge over the top and toward the back. The stems of these flowers should be significantly shorter than the larkspur, so the flowers nestle comfortably into the foliage. *Hydrangeas* are heavy drinkers, so be sure to insert the stems deep into the floral foam to ensure water uptake.

Add stock to the edge of the design in the gaps between the larkspur. These stems should be equal in length or slightly shorter than the larkspur. Position additional stock through the midsection and the top of the spray. Avoid filling the spaces immediately surrounding the *Hydrangea*.

Use linear stems of *Aster* 'Monte Cassino' among the larkspur and stock to enhance the oval outline. Then, add *Limonium* 'Misty Blue' to unify the floral components, still reserving space in the middle for the addition of focal flowers.

Use branched stems of *Eryngium* to add clusters throughout the spray, tucking some stems in deep and allowing others to extend to the tips of the design.

Position two or three fuji mums deep within the open spaces of the central focal area. Then, dot the design with additional fuji mums, keeping them well-spaced, including additions over the top and in the back.

Finish the spray with Oriental lilies placed within the focal area, near the surface of the design. Vary the facings of the lilies so the most central flowers look forward while others face upward, downward and toward the sides. Be sure to remove the lily anthers to prevent pollen from shedding and staining.

CASKET SPRAYS: ONE-SIDED OR ALL-AROUND?

There are different schools of thought on whether a casket spray should be designed one sided or all around. For most services in a church or funeral home, guests will observe the casket from only one side. In this case, the one-sided design is sufficient and can be made more affordable without extra flowers hidden in the back where no one will see them. However, at the cemetery, guests may gather on all sides of the casket, providing reason to add flowers to the back of the composition. The positioning of flower placements in a one-sided casket spray is typically more forward facing than in an all-around casket spray, in which flowers radiate in all directions. In the example above, the full-couch spray is designed in an all-around style. The vegetative full-couch variation and half-couch variation that follow are one sided.

Full-couch Spray Variation

Casket sprays are customarily designed with a low profile. This vegetative variation allows flowers to "grow" in parallel groups as they might be found in nature. The base of the design mimics the ground level of a garden, or in some designs, the forest floor. Mosses, berries and a variety of foliages create a natural setting while curly willow branches add height and create a frame that showcases the *Iris*, spray roses and *Freesia*. To alleviate transportation issues due to the height of this design, the florist must coordinate with the funeral director to determine who will transport the spray from the visitation or service to the burial site.

HALF-COUCH CASKET SPRAY

SUGGESTED MATERIALS:

Roses
Standard Carnations
'Green Trick' *Dianthus*
Stock
Liatris
Flat Fern
Leatherleaf Fern
Salal
Italian *Ruscus*
Seeded *Eucalyptus*
Flowering Cherry
Grapevine

The half-couch casket spray typically fills the space on the foot end of a half-open casket. A smaller version of the classic oval full-couch spray is appropriate for this use, but other design shapes are also possible. In this example, the half-couch spray is designed with asymmetrical balance, including a horizontal line of Liatris *and an offset cascade of Italian* Ruscus. *The left end of the spray is notably shorter than the right, which assures the flowers do not interfere with closing the lid or extend into the interior of the casket.*

DESIGN STEPS

1.

An OASIS® Small Casket Saddle provides a sturdy urethane base and caged floral foam wrapped in perforated poly film. Float the entire unit upside down in a tub of flower food solution until thoroughly soaked. Then, use salal to green up the saddle, starting with a short end on the left and a longer end on the right. Add stems of salal with downward angles at the corners and front edge.

2.

Create a horizontal line of flat fern across the base, extending the fern beyond the salal. Extend two to four stems of Italian *Ruscus* from the front left corner of the saddle in an arching downward cascade. Use short pieces of Italian *Ruscus* in the back right corner to establish a crescent line across the saddle.

3.

Use leatherleaf fern, and then additional flat fern, to green up the center of the saddle. Provide some lift to the center placements to create a mounded form.

4.

Add three or four *Liatris* to lengths comparable to the flat fern on the left. Repeat with seven or eight longer *Liatris* on the right. Allow the *Liatris* to radiate outward from the foam to broaden the horizontal lines. Use seeded *Eucalyptus* to connect the two groups of *Liatris* through the center.

5.

Use stock to create a diagonal line of opposition across the saddle, from the front right corner to the back left. Add a group of two or three more stock in the back right corner, then fill the vacant spaces of the design outline with carnations.

6.

Position five or six stems of 'Green Trick' *Dianthus* close to the foam in a zigzag pattern, from the front to the back through the center of the spray. Add four or five carnations among the *Dianthus*, extending them higher to enhance the mounded center.

7.

Complete the design with roses, starting with a trio in the center and extending them to the edges. Vary the flower facings so the center-most roses face forward and others angle up, down or to the side, based on their placement low, high or in the middle of the spray.

8.

Select flowering cherry branches with the desired lines to add graceful extensions beyond the outline of the spray. Use woody stems of grapevine (or portions of an unfurled grapevine wreath) across the top of the spray to unify the branches with the flowers. Insert one end of the grapevine into the foam, and weave it through the flowers to create a rhythmic pattern.

This classic mounded half-couch spray presents the flowers in a one-sided form, with stems bursting from the center outward. Linear materials including spiral *Eucalyptus*, *Gladiolus*, heather and lily grass contribute to the strong symmetrical rhythm. Football chrysanthemums add weight and balance while tulips and *Freesia* enhance the combination of flower forms and textures.

The waterfall design style has a graceful weeping quality that is well-suited to sympathy work. In this half-couch spray variation, flowers and foliage flow forward from the back of the casket saddle, creating a multilayered cascading composition. Linear materials, including callas, bells-of-Ireland, and spiral *Eucalyptus*, are placed first, followed by a center of mass and form flowers, with lily grass and curly willow tips providing the final filmy overlay. Textural variety, including the man-made tendrils of OASIS™ Rustic Wire, contributes to the appeal of this nature-inspired design.

CREMATION URN ARRANGEMENT

SUGGESTED MATERIALS:

Iris
Tulips
Ranunculus
Asters
Miniature *Hydrangea*
Heather
Hypericum
Bupleurum
Myrtle
Spiral *Eucalyptus*
Salal
Galax Leaves
Curly Willow
Sheet Moss

As cremations have increased as the preferred choice among individuals and families, so too have the options for the flowers that adorn the cremation urn during the memorial service. Arrangements that surround or embrace the urn provide comfort, candles add warmth, and branches provide shelter. While the size of cremation urn arrangements is notably smaller than casket designs, their impact is equally significant.

The proportions of a cremation urn arrangement can stretch comfortably to twice the height of the urn – and sometimes more – when branches or linear floral materials are used to extend it. Low and spreading designs are also appropriate and can be elongated into crescent or serpentine lines across the table surface on which the urn rests. When the urn is to be incorporated into the arrangement, care must be taken to assure the urn will be stable and is not marred when nestled among the floral materials.

DESIGN STEPS

1.

Fit an OASIS® Floral Foam Riser in a low dish or bowl, and secure with OASIS® Waterproof Tape. Use a vase or similar vessel atop the Styrofoam riser to mimic the cremation urn, which will be added upon delivery. Create a tall grouping of curly willow in the back left corner of the floral foam and a curvaceous accent in the front right corner. Place sheet moss randomly over about half of the floral foam and Styrofoam.

2.

Add myrtle and spiral *Eucalyptus* to form three vertical groupings of varied heights in the back, side and front edge of the foam, avoiding placements that obscure the urn. Supplement the base with additional short stems of the greens.

3.

Add stems of salal on each side of the urn extending horizontally beyond the container edge. Then, add a group of *Galax* leaves to the front right corner in an overlapping pattern that replicates its natural growth pattern.

4.

Use three or four *Iris* to establish a grouping taller than and to the left of the urn. Use six or seven tulips to create a shorter grouping among the *Galax* cluster on the right. Position each group of flowers so they appear to "grow" from a single point in the foam.

5.

Add a low grouping of miniature *Hydrangea* and asters beneath the *Iris* on the left. Use *Bupleurum* at the edges of the container in a meandering fashion, with breaks between groupings.

6.

Add plumes of heather to enhance the tulip patch. Then, establish a central focal area using *Ranunculus* and *Hypericum* berries in a low group that visually connects the tulips on the right with the *Iris* and asters on the left.

Larkspur, *Iris*, carnations and *Aster* in shades of violet harmonize peacefully with the chinoiserie-inspired urn. A floral foam wreath is cut in half to provide the foundation for the curved design. Seeded *Eucalyptus*, sheet moss and a variety of greens add texture and visual weight to the base while covering the wreath mechanics. Parallel flower placements in varying heights create a garden-like background to showcase the urn.

A bronze urn rests comfortably amid this garden of gold-toned flowers. Lilies and *Gerbera* are used in three positions to anchor the left, right and top of the arrangement while *Solidago* and button spray mums fill the gaps. Parallel stems of *Equisetum* support horizontal crossbars creating a trellis-like background that stops the eyes and keeps the attention on the urn.

A pair of matching cylinders form a bridge over a wooden cremation urn. White *Freesia*, roses and *Genista* complement the white containers while bells-of-Ireland, miniature *Hydrangea* and ivy provide the fresh green counterpoint. Curly willow and random spirals of bark wire suggest the wood tones of the urn. Rose petals sprinkled at the base visually connect the parts. This design might also be used to frame a portrait for a service with a closed casket.

EASEL SPRAY

Sympathy flower preferences vary regionally throughout the U.S., but in most communities, easel sprays are a well-accepted tribute option. Also known as a standing spray, these designs present the flowers in a forward-facing manner. It is important to develop dimension in the center of these designs to prevent a flat appearance. Typically, easel sprays are designed with an oval or diamond outline. Other variations include crescent and triangular shapes and contemporary line-mass designs.

Easels are most often made of heavy wire or lightweight wood. As a mechanical support, they should remain a background element in most finished designs. Exceptions are creations that involve enhancing or covering the easel with branches, bamboo, moss, foliage and the like. To transport an easel spray, fold the easel flat, with flowers attached, and lay the unit in the delivery vehicle.

SUGGESTED MATERIALS:

Roses

Carnations

Green and Variegated *Aspidistra* Leaves

Red Ti Leaves

Leatherleaf Fern

Plumosa Fern

Seeded *Eucalyptus*

OASIS™ Raw Muslin Ribbon

DESIGN STEPS

Soak a TRIBUTE CAGE® Holder in flower food solution, and secure it to an OASIS™ Wire Easel by hanging the cage from the eyelet on one of its ends onto the hook atop the easel. Use green chenille stems to secure the bottom corners of the holder to the legs of the easel so the cage will not rock. Use *Aspidistra* and red ti leaves to form a radiating oval outline, inserting the stems at the back edges of the holder and overlapping the leaves to create layers.

Use leatherleaf fern and then plumosa fern to fill in the center of the cage. These greens should extend forward 4 or 5 inches beyond the cage to create a slightly mounded form. Spray the foliage base with Floralife® Leaf Shine, if desired, for a glossy finish.

Arrange 10 to 12 standard carnations to create a vertical line from the top of the oval through the center to the base. Start with the first carnation 3 or 4 inches from the tips of the leaf outline. Stairstep the carnations, and decrease the spacing between them in the midsection of the spray, adding additional flowers to widen the center. The center-most carnations should extend forward just beyond the greens to continue the mounded form established by the greens.

Arrange about 10 additional carnations on the sides of the central line to create an oval outline. Allow generous spacing between these placements, and transition the flower facings so the longest flowers face upward, downward and to the sides of the spray.

Follow a process similar to Step 3 to create a vertical line of roses from the tip to the base of the spray, placing the roses in the vacant spaces between the carnations. Concentrate four or five roses close together in the center to develop the focal area.

Follow a process similar to Step 4, using roses to further define the oval outline. Pay careful attention to the overall outline of the flowers, stepping back to gain perspective, as needed. With the roses in place, the design shape should appear balanced and the spacing consistent.

Use seeded *Eucalyptus* to fill in the gaps, unify the carnations with the roses and add texture. Cut strips of muslin ribbon, and use them to form a pair of simple loops and streamers. Attach the ribbon to a wired wood pick, and insert near the focal area. Position the streamers so they fall gracefully to one side.

This modern easel spray variation features a large *Heliconia* wired to the exterior of the floral foam cage, allowing its hefty stem to form a dynamic line that is repeated by the *Gladiolus* and a central parade of *Gerbera*. Snapdragons and *Aspidistra* leaves break from the vertical line and provide an asymmetrical counterbalance. Loops of OASIS™ 3/16" Flat Wire enhance the visual rhythm while OASIS™ Natural Wrap Moss adds textural contrast.

SYMPATHY WREATH

The wreath, a symbol of eternity and the circle of life, is a classic sympathy flower option. Typically displayed on an easel, the sympathy wreath may be completely covered with flowers or designed with floral clusters and accents including ribbon, moss, and seasonal or personal accessories. A sash with script is sometimes used to identify the relationship of the deceased to the sender with sentiments such as "Beloved Grandmother" stated on the ribbon.

SUGGESTED MATERIALS:

Asiatic Lilies

Roses

Football Chrysanthemums

Daisy Spray (Pompon) Chrysanthemums

Miniature *Hydrangea*

Stock

Heather

Salal

Plumosa Fern

Floral foam wreath forms make it easy to design completely flower-covered wreaths while floral foam cages allow wreaths of grapevine, moss, ribbon-wrapped Styrofoam and others to be enhanced with flowers. The crescent form makes a highly suitable flower accent, following the curves and covering as much as two-thirds of the wreath base. Wreaths filled entirely with one flower type are referred to as monobotanical. Backgrounds of foliage or ribbon provide a tailored finish to these designs. Mixed compositions often reflect garden-inspiration. Here, instructions are provided for a mixed garden wreath featuring lilies, *Hydrangea*, roses, stock and chrysanthemums.

DESIGN STEPS

Insert short tips of salal into the interior and exterior perimeters of a soaked OASIS® Mâché Wreath base, overlapping placements to create a solid collar. Add short pieces of plumosa fern randomly to the top and sides of the wreath form.

Create three to six groups of stock, with rhythmic spacing around the wreath. Each group of stock should consist of two or three stems, used individually or cut into segments, and clustered on top and over the sides of the wreath.

Use feather or another linear filler to create tufted groupings by radiating several stems in different directions from common points in the foam. Make some groups larger than others, filling larger gaps with larger groups.

Place all the round flowers, one type at a time, in positions close to the foam so that some are on top of the wreath and others are on the inside or outside. Strive for consistent spacing so the weight and color of each flower is evenly distributed. Add the football mums first, followed by the miniature *Hydrangea*, daisy spray mums and roses.

Nestle the Asiatic lilies among the flowers in groups, allowing the lilies to rise slightly above the other flower types. Lily buds that extend above the flowers should be removed and inserted independently among the flower groupings. Add more stock, as needed, to fill remaining gaps and smooth out the rounded shape.

Attach the finished wreath to a wood easel using chenille stems or bark wire wrapped carefully and securely around the wreath and twisted around the easel posts that rise from the top. To prevent rocking, additional attachments can be made at the base of the wreath to secure the wreath to the easel legs.

An OASIS® Mâché Oval Wreath base provides the perfect foundation for this alternative wreath featuring a mostly monochromatic color harmony. Carnations and cushion spray mums fill the lion's share of the wreath, with miniature *Hydrangea* and segments of bells-of-Ireland completing the loop. Emphasis is achieved with *Ranunculus*, *Gerbera*, roses and *Freesia*, which add dimension and contrast. The circular rhythm is enhanced by the subtle transitions of flower types, and the weight is anchored by the dark centers of the *Gerbera*.

A grapevine wreath is naturally resplendent due to the generous and free-spirited use of greens and branches creating this woodland garden theme. An IGLU® Grande Holder supports the burst of tulips and *Freesia* at the base while a standard IGLU® Holder provides just enough floral foam to create an offset cluster on top. *Hypericum* and *Bupleurum* are the unifying filler elements. Loops and streamers of OASIS™ Raw Jute enhance the focal area and extend the line, resulting in greater perceived value.

This open-heart design achieves a clean and modern look by way of the simple patterned flower placements and a monochromatic color scheme. Two types of carnations, solid and variegated, are separated by the single row of forward-facing roses. The height difference between the roses and carnations create a perfect interior ledge to support the decorative wire accent.

HEARTS, CROSSES AND SET PIECES

When grieving a loss, loved ones often rely on symbols to communicate their emotions. Flowers designed in the shape of hearts, teardrops, pillows and crosses convey love, sadness, comfort and eternal life. These sympathy designs, typically ordered by family and friends, are displayed on easels. Smaller versions, when ordered by close relatives, may be displayed inside the casket lid.

Set pieces are flower-covered forms symbolizing the passions and interests of the deceased. A soccer ball, football or tennis racquet might be designed for a sports enthusiast; a guitar, keyboard or harp for a musician. Ballet slippers might be designed for a dancer; a shell or sea turtle for a beach lover. Cats, dogs, cows and horses are all requested from time to time. When designing set pieces with faces, care should be taken to avoid creating facial expressions that are excessively cheerful.

Florists must be innovative in engineering the foundations of these designs and creative in designing the colors and patterns of the flower placements. OASIS® Sculpting Sheets provide a means to cut a desired shape and design the flowers with a water source. Alternatively, Styrofoam can be used as a base, with the flowers pinned or glued in place.

This solid heart demonstrates the classic charm provided by a mixed combination of floral components. Standard carnations create a neatly defined outline that supports the interior sprinkled with *Gerbera*, roses, button spray mums and *Hypericum*. Baby's breath and a satin-and-sheer ribbon provide feminine finishing touches while the beads from OASIS™ MEGA Beaded Wire mimic tears of sadness.

Galax leaves, plumosa fern and Italian *Ruscus* establish a soft background for this peaceful cross. Standard carnations are lined up in rows to create the vertical and horizontal crossbars. Spiral *Eucalyptus* is used to establish the outline of a contrasting crescent-shaped accent. Tulips, heather and *Aster* 'Monte Cassino' fill out the center while OASIS™ Floral Cotton Lace Ribbon accentuates the cascading lines.